Business strategy
in practice

Business strategy in practice

Bengt Karlöf

Translated by Alan Gilderson

JOHN WILEY & SONS

Chichester · New York · Brisbane · Toronto · Singapore

Coventry University

PO 5402

British Library Cataloguing in Publication Data:

Karlöf, Bengt
  Business strategy in practice.
  1. Management
  I. Title II. Strategins Kärnfragor.
  English
  658   HD31
ISBN 0 471 91620 X

Library of Congress Cataloging-in-Publication Data:

Karlöf, Bengt, 1939–
  Business strategy in practice.

  Translation of: Strategins kärnfragor.
  1. Strategic planning. I. Title.
    HD30.28.K3613 1987   658.4'012   87–10452
ISBN 0 471 91620 X

Typeset by Inforum Ltd, Portsmouth
Printed and bound in Great Britain by
Courier International Ltd, Tiptree, Essex

Contents

6 Some typical strategic stituations

7 Key questions in strategy development processes

Appendix: The basics of strategy

Bibliography

Preface

The intention of this book is to fill a gap between the traditional academic literature on business and corporate strategy on one hand and the manager's reality in corporations on the other. For this English edition I have rewritten the book quite extensively as the niche carved out is apparently well related to the perceived needs. The literature in this field is, of course, dominated by Anglo-Saxon authors and in my opinion there are few attempts to tie the prevailing academic standard in this field to the actual needs of most companies, where management priority, of course, is to create efficiency in the strategy development process.

Probably the most dramatic change in the world of business today is the movement away from emphasis on the various concepts and techniques of business analysis and towards strategic leadership. A lively discussion is going on throughout the Western world, fuelled by the shortage of strategically thinking corporate executives and the undue importance attached to business analysis in general and quantitative anlaysis in particular.

In the course of my work as a consultant at Indevo I have been privileged to witness the ongoing replacement of one paradigm by another – a change that has broadened the perspective from the limitations and explanatory models of traditional management science. It is natural for business executives and consultants in the forefront of the battle to take a keen interest in the phenomena, inexplicable in terms of traditional management philosophy, that have emerged in the past decade.

I hope that this book will contribute to the body of knowledge on which training in and development of the new views will be founded – views that have emerged from empirical business experience and will naturally be worked up into more scientific models in the future. Those models will hopefully be better able to explain what we are now witnessing.

I have decided not to cite sources or founts of inspiration for all the ideas expressed here, though many of them, naturally, are derived from the thinking and experience of others. This does not reflect any desire to strut in borrowed plumage, but is simply intended to make the book more readable. I take sole responsibility for the structuring and reintegration of ideas, both others', and my own.

I hope that you and other readers will continue to supply me with constructive suggestions for improvement from your own experience.

Bengt Karlöf
Stockholm, 27th March, 1987

Outline of the book

This book gives a personal and concise yet complete review of the subject of business strategy and its current status in theory and practice. It is intended to give the reader such a grasp of the structre, terminology and process of strategy that he or she will be able to play an effective part in, or lead, a process of strategic change in a company.

Chapter 1: Strategic management

The introductory chapter explains why a demand for strategic management capability has now arisen. Strategy development was formerly controlled to a large degree by the planning function. The essence of the change that is now taking place – usually signalled by the use of the term 'strategic management' – is that business sense controls the work of planning instead of the other way around.

The chapter further explains why the need for strategic management capability has grown so markedly in recent years, describing and defining the strategic management capabilites that may be required of managers and executives as a result of the new emphasis on drive, business sense and a holistic view.

A section on trade logic illustrates the special importance of business sense. The hallmarks of strategic management include knowledge of and feeling for the market, the customers, and the structures of need that create customer demand.

Chapter 2: Concepts and structure of strategy

The second chapter deals with the central concepts that occur in all literature and all discussions on the subject of strategy. The intention is not to impart any new significance to expressions already in use, but rather to specify the meanings usually assigned to these expressions. The presentation is more extensive on some points than on others, for example on the concept of corporate mission. As a result of my own background in the field of business development, I have worked a great deal with that particular concept and therefore lean heavily towards an interpretation based on need and demand, rather than the wider interpretation encompassing a large element of inward corporate life.

The importance of vision, both as a yardstick of development and as a source of motivation in the organization, is considered an an overriding concept in the visualization of goals.

The term 'goal' and 'level of ambition' are used as interchangeable synonyms in this book. Some other terms are sometimes used in two senses. One example is 'market strategy', which can mean either business strategy or marketing strategy. However, the sense in which such terms are used will always be apparent from the context.

The section headed 'The elements of strategy' is my way of describing in concrete terms the separate components that go to make up a business strategy. Whereas the rest of the chapter can be regarded as a compilation and interpretation of terms in current use, the section on the elements of strategy is an attempt to make a personal contribution to practical work with strategies.

Chapter 3: The strategic process – vision, understanding the business and analysis

There has been a continuing increase in the amount of attention paid to the actual implementation of strategies. In practice, this has happened to such a degree that goal formulation and analysis have been overshadowed – so much so that analysis has come to be regarded with disfavour in many situations. The aim of the chapter is to give a concrete presentation of the successive stages in a process of strategy development. The elements of the model are naturally not new, but I take sole personal responsibility for the sequence (chronological order) and total concept. One important observation I have made is that the difference between portfolio strategy and business strategy is not clearly understood among company executives, even though a clear distinction between the two is made in practically all the literature on strategy.

Determining the level of ambition of the leading persons involved is a cornerstone of any process of strategy development. I have chosen to assign the determination of this level of ambition to what I have called the analysis phase of the process – a choice that can be questioned, as can my assignment of strategy determination to the subsequent implementation phase (in Chapter 4). The reason why I have opted for this particular structure is that determining the level of ambition is a fundamental yet often neglected variable that is of crucial importance to the rest of the process.

Chapter 4: The strategic process – determination of strategy and implementation

As for strategy determination, this is not in my opinion a natural deductive step in the analytical process, but something that calls for business experience and, above all, creativity, to a degree that has not always been realized.

Creativity is a word that has been widely misused, as it has developed into one of those managerial buzz-words. Creativity in business means the ability to combine established elements of knowledge into innovative patterns, thereby improving competitive capability. Being creative thus requires elements of knowledge that are in turn gathered through analysis and experience.

Implementation and its implications represent one of the recent advances in the field of strategy. It is difficult to capture the whole complexity of a process of implementation on paper; in Chapter 4 I have tried to set down some of the main points of vital importance, together with some of the pitfalls that we have been able to observe in real-life situations.

Chapter 5: Strategies for business development

Business development and the strategies devised for it are really only a special case of the strategic approach. Business development is specifically characterized by concentration on the revenue-generating aspects, with less emphasis on economies of scale and productivity. These latter concepts can be said to have dominated earlier strategic thinking. This is not to say that the benefits of large-scale operation and productivity are not important: far from it. My own personal background is that I have worked extensively in business development in the sense of generation of business, both creating new businesses and restructuring existing ones. I have accordingly found it natural to include a chapter on theoretical models for business development, especially as this is an area of immediate interest to many companies.

Chapter 6: Some typical strategic situations

In any company or organization there are a number of typical situations that are often used as means of implementing a strategy. Increasing capacity and establishing new outlets are a couple of examples. Another common situation, one controlled by outside circumstances, is the deregulation of industries. This has happened for example to airline travel and air freight in Europe, and to banking in many countries. The aim of the chapter is to consider a number of typical situations of this kind and identify their characteristics in a way that will help the reader faced with similar situations in his own industry or his own company.

Chapter 7: Key questions in strategy development processes

The final chapter of the book raises a series of issues which are highly relevant to strategy development processes but do not fall directly under any of the other chapter heads. One might of course attempt to broaden the framework of the strategic process to include *everything*, but in that case a division into chapters would be meaningless. I have therefore chosen to list a number of isolated items for consideration in this last chapter.

I would like to take this opportunity of acknowledging the ideas and experience contributed by many practical businessmen and businesswomen with whom I have spoken. This kind of feedback is always valuable, so if you, dear reader, have anything in your own experience that you feel might be of general interest, I would be glad if you would write to me care of the publishers. Perhaps we can help each other to advance the state of the art of strategy.

1 Strategic management

What is the essence of strategic ability?

The object of any exercise in business strategy is to locate, attract and keep customers, i.e. buyers of the goods and/or services your company supplies. The starting point must be a deep and genuine understanding of the customer needs which you are satisfying and which generate the demand that supplied your earnings. Without this insight, management thinking is isolated from the world the company lives in. This kind of isolation has existed in many companies, but has been concealed by the technocratic attitude to management that seemed to work before the paradigm shift of the mid-1970s. This definition implies that work with portfolio strategies, i.e. with groups of business units, is an entirely different matter. We shall return to that aspect later.

Most companies realize the need for change, at least intellectually. Modern management literature and executive schooling strongly and rhetorically emphasize the need for innovation, visionary thinking and leadership. All too often, however, the response is inadequate because radical thinking is in such a short supply, and conservative thinking so strongly entrenched, that any incipient change tends to diffuse into the system.

> Traditional attempts at strategy development have obstructed the development of knowledge necessary to successful businessmanship.

This statement may seem outrageous, but I shall explain it in a moment. I believe that by applying operations research, experience curves, simplified matrices based on market shares and other techniques of planning technocracy, managements have in fact studiously avoided acquiring the knowledge that is most essential to successful businessmanship, namely knowledge of trade logic and the structure of customer needs. Representatives of corporate strategy

6

expertise have thus focused attention on reflections of what is essential, and in doing so have wrongly focused it on symptoms instead of causes.

One reason for this may be the high-speed career pattern to which graduate engineers, economists and other highly educated individuals in companies are exposed. The earlier belief in the universal applicability of general management skills ignored the importance of understanding trade logic.

Expressions like 'back to basics' can generally be interpreted as reflecting a new realization of how important basic businessmanship is.

The term 'trade logic' naturally needs to be defined and explained if it is not to become just another management buzz-word. You will find a definition and discussion of this fundamental concept at the end of this chapter.

Strategy in many companies was formerly handled by central 'strategic planning units'. Economic development after the Second World War was, if not entirely linear, at least fairly predictable in many industries, with the result that the planning methods used seemed to work with high precision. This being so, various planning techniques tended so to speak to gain ascendancy over business instinct, so that strategy in many cases was left entirely in the hands of corporate planning departments.

The change that we can now see taking place is a move away from planning methods as the most important part of strategy. Business sense is taking their place as the dominant factor. This does not in any way imply that planning is being scrapped altogether, but it does imply a distinct shift of standpoint in that businessmanship has been elevated to a commanding position in the work of strategy, while the planning function has been assigned an auxiliary role.

The dramatic aspect of the shift that is taking place lies in the way the need for strategic management ability has expanded. This kind of ability is now required of many more individuals in the corporate organization; above all, it is an ability that must exist in the individual profit centres, no matter whether they are called subsidiaries or divisions. This shift of emphasis further implies, as I have said above, an upgrading of buinessmanship in the operative units and a relative downgrading of the perceived importance of staff-work to success in business.

The new realization of the need for business skill to control the development of strategy has however led to some overreaction. One of the consequences has been a drastic decline in the status of the planning function. This is regrettable insofar as planning and progamming are necessary components of the processing of strategy development. The essence of the new approach, however, is that business acumen should control planning, and not the other way around. Operations research is an effective planning instrument for optimization within the framework of a *given* scenario. Strategy development, on the other hand, often involves evaluation of *different* scenarios. Business acumen, as applied for example to identification of key strategic factors, must be the prime requisite for establishing the scenario which in turn will provide the basis for subsequent planning.

One of the reasons why the planning function has fallen into disrepute is the overcapacity that resulted from extrapolation of economic trends in the late 1960s and early 1970s. In many cases, and in a large number of industries, this overcapacity had disastrous consequences which naturally coloured judgements made in hindsight.

A further background variable has influenced conditions in my own country, Sweden. On top of the energy crisis that touched off the ongoing reappraisal of the work of strategy development, Sweden was hit by an 'excess cost crisis' during the 1970s. Its roots lay in the pay raises averaging 19.5% per annum in 1973, 1974 and 1975. This excess cost crisis, coming as it did on top of the energy crisis, meant that the rethinking of strategy in Sweden had to be much more radical than in most other countries. We are now reaping the fruits of that rethinking, which among other things has led to a healthy shakeout in industry and a rise in the general level of management skill. In addition, the dual crisis forced Sweden into an immediate recognition of how much it depended on the outside world. That is one of the main reasons why the new approach to strategy has been adopted so quickly and been relatively far-reaching in Sweden.

What is strategic management

I shall now give a five-point definition of strategic management. It consists of the ability to:

1. see *patterns* in what is happening;
2. identify *need for change*;

3. devise *strategies* for change;
4. provide *tools* for change;
5. resolutely *implement* strategies for change.

1 Seeing patterns

The terms 'holistic vision' and 'helicopterability' often refer to the ability to recognize the interplay between customer needs, customer demand, competitors and their products, and one's own company and its ability to satisfy customers' needs in interaction with these and other forces. Defined in this way, analysis is obviously a fundamental part of strategic thinking. But the complexity and breadth of variations of the analysis make it difficult to reduce to models. The greater the business strategist's ability to abstract, the more clearly the relationships of the business pattern emerge. The ability to go from concretion to abstraction and back again is thus an important aspect of strategic competence. By using this ability one can grasp patterns in the environment that can be used to trace the need for change in one's own company.

2 Identifying the need for change

Changes in companies nowadays take place in many more dimensions than used to be the case. For most companies, change was formerly to all intents and purposes synonymous with expansion. Changes are composed of a many-faceted set of variables ranging from cost effectiveness in production to differentiation of the product range; they also involve many 'soft' factors like questions of quality and attitudes to risk-taking. Identification of a need for change calls for two abilities:

●   being alert to trends arising out of *known factors* in the industry in question;
●   using one's intelligence and creativity to try to *combine known and unknown variables* and thereby to achieve a state of readines for unforeseen contingencies and recognize opportunities to improve the company's ability to compete.

The easy but inadequate solution, of course, is to predict that the situation tomorrow will be the same as it is today. We all have an innate tendency to take 'just like now only more so' as our model for assessing the future.

3 Devising strategies

Strategy determination, or strategy formulation as it is sometimes called, is both an intellectual process, a process of winning acceptance and a creative process. Large parts of this book deal specifically with strategy determination. One essential factor is the need to secure understanding of the structure of the strategy within that part of an organization or company for which you have the responsibility of developing strategies. Another is the actual process of implementation and understanding of its component elements.

4 Tools for change

Knowledge of the components of strategic management and some knowledge of traditional attitudes to questions of strategy are excellent aids to good management. Most strategy models are constructed on a foundation of operations research which, to the new way of thinking, makes them suspect. But, if nothing else, a good all-round education in strategics should include a knowledge of both the old and new BCG (Boston Consulting Group) matrices, McKinsey's 7S, the experience curve, etc. (see the review of such models in the Appendix). Some of the models of this type, such as PIMS (profit impact of market strategy, about which I will have more to say in Chapter 3, p. 72 ff.), still have an impressive explanatory value, especially in certain sections of strategic analysis.

5 Implementing strategies

All the mental effort and creativity you put into devising a strategy will be so much waste of time unless you can put your ideas into effect. This apparently obvious statement has not in fact been obvious for so very long, which explains why I may sometimes seem to place exaggerated emphasis on the implementation aspect. Conversely, action unsupported by a structure of thought is usually fairly pointless. Running at high speed without first deciding where you want to get to is generally just as ineffective as high-powered thinking that is not followed by action.

Structure and dynamism, in other words, are the two essentials that must be paired to bring any proposed change to a successful conclusion.

With the definition of strategic management that I have adopted, a major problem becomes evident right from the outset. Traditional Western business philosophy leans heavily towards maximizing short-term profits and eliminating risks. A most difficult problem connected with the chosen definition, as with all work in strategy, is that of finding ways to measure the effects of strategic management ability and to set rewards commensurate with the resulting changes. This applies especially to operations in investment-intensive industries where turnaround times are long and the effects do not become apparent for quite a while.

'By their fruits ye shall know them.' In most organizations, the 'fruits' are the operative results. Most executives are promoted up the organizational ladder on the basis of their operational accomplishments, so it is not hard to understand why career patterns and the demand for results so heavily influence current criteria for success in business.

One great problem is that executives in general do not receive training in strategic leadership and therefore do not develop their strategic thinking to keep pace with their advancement in the corporate hierarchy. There is a great deal to be said for revising the criteria for success as executives climb higher up the career ladder. They need to have their strategic thinking ability exercised by being given opportunities to study different strategic situations. An average chief executive may only encounter two or three strategic situations in his whole career. It is an often overlooked fact that strategic management ability depends in no small degree on this very kind of strategic experience. Creating or simulating opportunities for strategic thinking is thus an important factor in leadership development.

Strategic management ability

Closely associated with the foregoing remarks on strategic experience is the question of how to judge whether a person is capable of strategic management. Practical operative skills, however valuable they may be, are not always accompanied by the corresponding strategic skills.

To avoid any risk of misunderstanding, I want to emphasize the value of operative ability. There are examples of able, energetic individuals who have built up large companies without possessing any particular gifts for strategy. It is no accident that there is now a growing demand for strategic management ability. The reason is, of course, that the need for this kind of ability increases with the growth of competition. In my capacity as a consultant I still see how individuals with operative skills do well in new growth industries without benefit of strategic management ability.

The winners in these growth industries are eventually singled out when the growth curve flattens and strategic management ability is put to the test.

> The computer games industry mushroomed during the second half of the 1970s, and people with a nose for business and a willingness to take risks made plenty of money out of it for a few years. Most of the companies went to the wall when the expansion levelled out, except for those with managements capable of strategic thinking.
>
> From Sweden we have the example of engineering consultancy, a business that grew rapidly in the wake of the build-up of the country's infrastructure. When growth stopped and a peiod of structural change set in, consultancy firms found their strategic management ability put to the test.
>
> The competitive climate grew much harsher, and leadership began to pass from managments characterized primarily by engineering expertise to managements of alert businessmen. As always when an industry enters its plateau phase, there was also a shift in the structural pattern as managements of a more strategic turn of mind began to buy up less business-oriented firms in the profession.

Thus strategic ability is not put to the test until conditions arise where the competitive climate calls forth business skills.

How shall we define and measure strategic management ability? Latter-day research has supplied some criteria for judging the aptitude and capacity of individuals for succeeding in business strategy. Here are some of the traits commonly found in individuals who are likely to be good strategists:

- A capacity for *lateral or inductive thinking*, i.e. the ability to pursue bold, unconventional trains of thought that link elements of knowledge to each other in new ways.
- *Conceptual thinking*, i.e. the ability to proceed from the concrete to the abstract and thence back to a concrete reality.
- *Holistic vision*, i.e. the ability to see the whole without being confused or constrained by the parts, or, in more simple terms, to see the wood and not just the trees:
- *Expressiveness*, i.e. the ability to translate abstract thinking about a business situation into clear, communicative images capable of convincing other people.
- *Foresight*, i.e. the willingness and ability to allow for future events and trends as an important dimension in

the formulation of strategy. This need not involve thinking ahead to the next Ice Age, but simply trying to envisage some possible future scenarios.

I should like to develop some of the foregoing points in more detail.

At the mention of foresight and assessment of the future we are all apt to imagine some kind of galactic forecast including everything from a change of government in China to the exhaustion of the earth's manganese reserves. There is a danger of getting caught up in woolly visions of the future that have no bearing on the business in hand. All contingency planning must of course be relevant to one's own operations.

Developments in airfreight during the second half of the 1970s and the first half of the 1980s offer a good example. Supply in that business is governed not by its own demand but by demand in another business – that of carrying passengers. The introduction of wide-bodied aircraft on scheduled international routes in the mid 1970s was prompted by increased demand for passenger-carrying capacity. But since aircraft fuselages are circular in cross-section, cargo space increased with the square of the radius. This resulted in a huge surplus of freight-carrying capacity, which in turn led to price-cutting.

At the same time many airlines were investing in special freighter aircraft for trans-Atlantic and trans-Pacific service!

The whole civil aviation industry was a growth sector up to the mid-1970s, but one in which strategic thinking was conspicuous by its absence. The build-up of airfreight capacity can serve as a good example of what happens when no attention whatsoever is paid to what is going to happen in the future, even things that can be foreseen at the time the dicussions are in progress.

Shipbuilding is another example. A colleague who worked in the Swedish shipbuilding industry at the beginning of the 1970s was fully aware of the expansion plans of yards in Japan, South Korea and other countries. The information was all there, but evidently there was no strategic discussion of what effect this expansion would have on the Swedish shipbuilding industry. A giant dock designed for the building of giant vessels was commissioned at Uddevalla in 1974; the project was pushed through by highly placed politicians in a situation where the facts about the world shipbuilding industry's expansion plans were plain for all to see.

A question of fundamental interest in discussing strategic management ability is the importance of creativity to excellent strategy formulation as opposed to analysis and deductive thinking, i.e. the drawing of conclusions in logical sequences. At an accelerating pace in recent years, research has elucidated human capabilities and limitations in various respects. To simplify somewhat, the discussion has been about mathematical ability and organizational skills in contrast to creativity and holistic vision. Although many over-simplified interpretations have been bandied about in this somewhat faddish debate, the arguments do nevertheless have a high explanatory value that many people have experienced as a tangible reality.

The whole educational system of the Western world has been roundly criticized for tending to reward only deductive rationality, i.e. organized, derivable logic. The result of this bias in favour of analytical ability has been that inductive abilities – entrepreneurship, business instinct, creativity, etc. – have come to be regarded as characteristics to be penalized rather than rewarded.

New thinking in business management and the growth of 'management science' are largely concerned with the balance between traditional analysis and rational thinking on the one hand and the newly discovered business instinct and creativity on the other. Today there are signs that the pendulum has swung too far the other way, with a tendency to deprecate analysis. Well-known men and women have maintained that analysis is only a very small part of successful strategy development, which is very largely a matter of implementation. This may be partly true, especially in companies that produce services, but is largely untrue in many other, more industrial types of business. The swing of the pendulum towards action has been educationally beneficial, but could in the long run be qualitatively harmful.

Traditional strategy models are based on analysis, while the new thinking seeks a balance and interaction between analysis, creativity and entrepreneurship, i.e. between thought, feeling and action. The most elusive aspect of strategy is the true importance of dynamism to success. Tempo has been inceasingly recognized as a success factor, and this dynamism does not lend itself to description by analytical models.

Henry Mintzberg has the following to say about deductive analytical models:

> '[This hypothesis] would help to explain why each of the new analytic techniques of planning and analysis has, one after the other, had so little success at the policy level. PBBS, strategic planning, 'management' (or 'total') information systems, and

models of the company – all have been greeted with great enthusiasm; then, in many instances, a few years later have been quietly ushered out the corporate back door. Apparently none served the needs of decision making at the policy level in organizations; at that level other processes may function better.'

People in all ages have tried to find explanatory models to capture the most complex events and make them comprehensible. Before Copernicus and Kepler, astronomers tried to explain the movements of the planets on the basis of a geocentric cosmology – and very nearly succeeded. It is the same forces, of course, that lie behind rational man's dream of the comprehensive decision-making model that will encompass the complexity of a company in all its breadth. The performance of decision-making models in real life has been unsatisfactory, for the same reason that people with proven track records of success in business almost never win business games: the winners are those whose talents lie in 'beating the system', i.e. those who grasp the technicalities that control the outcome of the games.

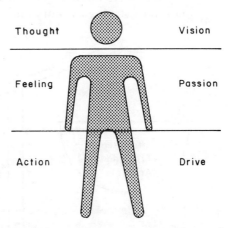

Fig. 1 Thought, feeling and action – essential ingredients of strategic management

Let us return for a moment to foresight. The strategic thinkers, those gifted with curiosity, acumen and sensitivity, are the quickest to detect the first signs of change. They redirect their strategies, redeploy their resources, reprogram their development projects, etc. The more ponderous and less sensitive ones fall behind and risk finding themselves in an environment where:

● overcapacity is universal;

15

- competition from newly industrialized countries is strong and growing;
- all the technology is for sale, the market is in a state of war and the possibilities for differentiation are non-existent;
- winners become losers overnight.

This applies not only to companies but also to nations, regions, industries and private individuals. So foresight and fast reflexes cannot be overemphasized as prime qualities in strategic management.

Finally, I want to emphasize the drive to compete and make money. Entrepreneurship, in combination with strategic ability, is an important success factor. What I am talking about here is businessmanship in the sense of a powerful motivation for one or more dominant individuals who want to improve the competitive position of their own company. In contrast to the case of administration-oriented management, this means that the energy and drive exist to push development forward instead of just 'managing' the company's operations. In business development, the combination of strategic ability and ability to act is unbeatable.

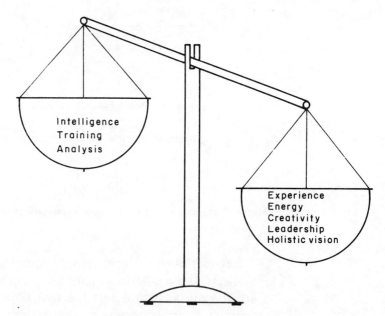

Fig. 2 Reappraisal of leadership qualities. A certain amount of rethinking is now being done as to what are the most important qualities for general leadership in business. Less importance is being attached to the old virtues like intelligence, education, dress and pedigree, and more to initiative, experience, energy and creativity. The movement is slower in large corporations, but the trend can be clearly discerned.

Trade logic: an essential tool for the strategist

In the new business-oriented school of strategy which is beginning to emerge – and which I support – many of the earlier models are regarded as attempts to achieve realistic simplifications without the need to go into the specific trade logic of each industry. In view of the former basis of strategic work in companies and organizations, it is easy to understand why this approach has predominated.

If your primary aim is to strike a balance in a portfolio, i.e. a group of business units more or less related to each other, it is naturally difficult to make an indepth study of the trade logic of each of the different industries represented in the portfolio – and strategy development from the 1950s onward has proceeded from the basic standpoint of portfolio strategy. In more recent times there has been a shift via the concept of strategic business units to a consideration of the problems of business strategies, or competitive strategies, which call for skills in businessmanship rather than in portfolio management.

Businessmanship demands a knowledge of trade logic and a will to compete.

Portfolio strategy demands a stuctural analysis to strike an optimum balance in a portfolio on the basis of divided resources and synergies.

This, then, is the background to the move towards giving a higher priority to understanding a trade logic, which is what this section is about. Comparatively little attention was paid to the logic that applied to individual industries during a period totally dominated by interest in portfolio strategies. Now that interest in business strategies is growing, people have tried to substitute various attempts at operations analysis for in-depth knowledge of trade logic. And widespread efforts are still being made to find the keys to success by seeking and finding statistical correlations. In my opinion it is futile to try and do this without understanding the reasons why such correlations exist.

17

Definition of trade logic

The term 'trade logic' may seem pompous and vague, so perhaps I had better define it more rigorously be specifying its components.

Components of trade logic

(a) Structure of needs and changes in demand.

(b) The product that satisfies the needs.

(c) Degree of 'product mystique'.

(d) Users/distributors and suppliers and the interactions between them.

(e) Segments of the market and strategic groups.

(f) Profitability and the importance of the industry to society.

The key to success in business is unquestionably to be found in a deep understanding of the *underlying stuctures of customer needs* and the demand that those needs generate. There is a law, Say's law, which says:

Supply creates demand.

What Say is actually trying to tell us is that the nature of demand is not preordained by fate but can be influenced by available supply. Needs, on the other hand, are more constant. Let us take an example:

The demand for personal computers (PCs) is certainly determined to a large degree by the simplification of work that their use offers. I believe, however, that the demand for PCs is determined to an even larger degree by the prestige motive associated with the common human need to seem important and successful. When I reiterated that belief several times in the course of a recent lecture, a member of the audience drew my attention to a study by Apple Computers that had confirmed this very point.

In this case, then, the underlying need can be identified as the need to project an image of success. That need could conceivably be satisfied through a demand for turbo cars, mobile telephones or personal computers. The supply of PCs has thus created a demand that is not rationally based. The manufacturer of PCs who understands the structure of the demand, and the nature of the need that underlies it, is much more likely to succeed because he can appeal directly to the real need, thereby satisfying it better and boosting demand for his own particular products.

Those of us in business who are economists, engineers and the like by training have a tendency to project our own rationality on to customers in a given industry and assume that they behave in a totally rational manner.

The rationality trap

The tendency to believe that our customers are as rational as we are.

In the 1970s, when it was taken for granted – at least in Europe – that everything was done on rational grounds, the car of the future was spoken of as a 'transporter cube'. This discussion led to a marked neglect of values that were important to car buyers. One result was that the 'customer-perceived quality' of cars declined (because the manufacturers eschewed ornamentation). Another was that people with a different and more catholic view of what constituted quality in cars turned to countries like the USA where their view was shared.

In the case of airfreight there is of course a rational need to improve profitability by taking advantage of fast transportation to cut down the amount of captial tied up in operations. A decision by a company to use an airfreight service ought naturally to be based on that rational motive.

An airfreight carrier, however, is much less likely to succeed in business if he fails to realize that in many people's minds the idea of airfreight is charged with a dynamic, action-filled aura that gives an impression of much greater speed and precision than is found in real life.

This last example illustrates another point, which is that different target groups can have widely different motives for demanding the same product. The customers of the airfreight industry are mostly shipping managers who are paid not primarily for their ability to minimize the capital commitments of the companies who employ them, but rather for their ability to negotiate the cheapest possible freight rates, or possibly to secure a certain regularity and precision in the flow of goods.

In such a situation, the rational person is all to apt to fall into the 'rationality trap' by assuming that shipping managers act in a rational manner from their employers' point of view. He is tempted to draw up uniform marketing strategies that are not optimal because they do not take account of varying patterns of demand.

> The ability to understand customers and the needs that underlie demand is a new dimension of strategy development that calls for 'business competence'.

The next component of trade logic is the *product*, i.e. the mix of goods and services used to satisfy needs and create demand. Say's law (supply creates demand) naturally applies here. It is quite conceivable that some new product in the sphere of turbo cars, PCs and mobile telephones might arise to create a demand that satisfies the underlying structure of need, and that such a product might steal market shares, so to speak, from those other products. It is not unrealistic to imagine that 'electronic mail', or other modern means of communication that make the user look progressive and dynamic, could emerge as a competitor in this market. There are studies which show that demand for status symbols of that kind in the executive world is in inverse proportion to success in that same world.

One of the most important reasons why understanding of trade logic is such a fundamental variable is that you can utilize it to adjust your supply of goods and services so that it matches the underlying structure of customer needs better than it does now – and hopefully better than your competitors' do now.

The degree of *product mystique* is associated with the need-demand-supply complex. The term 'product mystique' refers to the importance of the factors that make the value of a product more a function of image than of economy or technology. If we consider perfume as an example of the one extreme, where the value of the product lies almost entirely in its image, i.e. in social perception of its reality, then we can take standard quality steel I-girders as an example of the other extreme. If you cannot create an aura of mystery around the product itself, you have to create one round the supplier, the delivery system, or something else associated with it.

In many industries it is usual to look for differentiation variables, i.e. the factors that create a special distinction, in the product itself. Manufacturers of hand-held power drills often promote them by claiming higher speed, lower operating cost or more footage. But more and more industries are finding that they can no longer differentiate the product itself. Their competitor's products do exactly the same things that theirs do, reducing their ability to claim any special distinction in terms of customer needs. Especially in the engineering industries there is a tendency to go on investing, and even to increase investment, in product development in an effort to find differentiation variables that will give them a competitive edge.

In my view, they would often be better advised to try and find differentiation variables that could give them a competitive edge in a much wider area. This applies particularly to engineering companies, who for natural reasons have a tradition of despising any aspect not directly related to the technical performance of the product.

A phenomenon that often occurs as products grow more commodity-like is that dealers begin to appear on the scene. Their interest in product-related differentiation is often low, and 'dealer technology' often differs widely in terms of need from that of users.

The foregoing reasoning brings us to another component of trade logic, the *interaction between users, distributors and suppliers*. The assignment of roles and the importance of individual factors varies with time according to the state of maturity of the industry. In mature industries we often find the problem of overcapacity, which leads to concentration on price competition. A modern view of strategy based on the total structure of customer needs offers much greater opportunities of operating at a profit even in a mature industry.

A *segment* of a market can be defined as a part of the total market whose needs differ in some respect from those of the market as a whole. In the total passenger car market there is a need for both Fiats and Volvos and Jaguars, and the segments of the market are often matched by strategic groups of suppliers who concentrate on specific segments. When I mentioned airfreight earlier I touched on the different structures that exist in a market. There *are* target groups in the total population with particular needs, and an understanding of those needs naturally makes it easier for the individual company to determine its strategy.

The *profitability of an industry and its importance to the business community and society at large* can throw a valuable light on the work of strategy. Back in the 1920s the steel industry was of decisive importance to the development of society, just as the computer industry is today. The methods of competition used in the steel industry nowadays are very different from those used in the 1920s, and it is safe to predict that methods of competition in the computer industry will undergo equally great changes in the future.

The steel industry today is of relatively little importance to society. Its technology is well established and familiar. The steel industry is suffering from an embarrasing over-capacity. This has created quite different intellectual premises in connection with strategy determination, and has marked effects on the management resources available.

The observant reader will have noted that the various components of trade logic have a common denominator composed of need structures, demand and supply. It is of course no coincidence that these very components, together with competitors and substitutes, constitute the building blocks of the corporate mission of a business enterprise. Understanding of trade logic is far from being simply a deductive process that can be applied with the help of ordinary analytical tools. It is very much a process based on empathy, creativity, and that variety of analysis which is called intuition, i.e. the ability to put together a large number of fragments of information and to draw conclusions from them without being able to explain the logic that led to those conclusions.

Frederick Gluck, Vice President of McKinsey, has said that though there is now a strategic frame of reference, all too often the work of strategic development is controlled by intellectual and rigid analyses and steps rather than by sensititivity and flexibility in the business environment. This, he says, is one of the chief reasons why the clients of consultant firms grow incrementally and find it hard to achieve the radical reorientation they often badly need.

It is easy to fail to identify a competitive edge when going through the mechanical motions of a planning process. Forecasts of costs and prices are irrelevant compared with trade logic and the structure of business.

Strategy and corporate values

Business strategies for a business unit aim at achieving external efficiency. By this I mean a set of elements which together aim at making the business unit more competitive.

22

A company has certain collective values, and it is most important to take these into account when formulating its strategy. There are of course any number of qualities that can be prized, but the basic values or virtues of importance to success in business are:

- hard work;
- risk-taking, rewards and penalties;
- energy, drive and initiative;
- intelligence and training;
- respect for human beings as a resource in general, and for employees in particular as contributors to success;
- recognition that customers and their needs are the point upon which business turns.

The expression 'corporate culture' is generally used to refer to the attitudes, opinions and behaviour patterns through which these basic values are expressed. Corporate culture can be considered to be a manifestation of the values that are expressed in and influence such things as organizational stucture and personnel selection.

The hallmark of 'excellent' companies (a term coined by Petes and Waterman) is a symbiosis between business strategy and corporate culture. Deep involvement and devotion to one's work are often inward criteria for success in business.

During the 1950s and 1960s a belief grew up in a technocratic approach to business management. The theory behind this belief was that management was a matter of technique, a standard component that could be plugged into any company in any industry.

Excellence studies have shown that the technocratic approach to business management has not been nearly as successful as the approach based on deep involvement and a strong feeling for the business.

With the growing importance of the peripheral service factor as a criterion for customers' choice of suppliers, the association of strategy with corporate values and culture has become more vital then ever. Strategic management ability must embody a strong sense of values and culture; strategy can no longer be considered in isolation from the inward life of a company.

2 Concepts and structure of strategy

Why is the terminology of strategy so difficult?

During its lifetime the concept of strategy has undergone a radical metamorphosis. It has sloughed off its old 'planning skin' to reveal its present and still shiny-new 'management skin'. Having formerly borrowed approaches and models from the taxonomy of planning, strategy is now swinging towards businessmanship. This has not exactly helped to reduce the number of terms or clarify their significance.

It is also important to remember that all the well-known strategy models have their origins in the 'old paradigm', i.e. they all derive from planning-oriented strategy analysis. In this book I have deliberately refrained from reviewing all the existing analytical models, assuming that the reader knows of them. For reference, a discussion of some of the main models is given in the Appendix. The model that stands out as possibly the most 'business-like' is PIMS; though it too derives from operations research, it also makes allowance for a number of 'soft' variables like relative product quality. It is moreover founded on an empirically constructed database.

There is no scientifically accepted 'best model' that can be thrust upon all companies. This is still an experimental science, so there are no universally acknowledged models, concepts or structures to go on.

Yet there is always a ready market for a tool that holds out the promise of being able to capture a broad complexity in one all-embracing model. In companies, as everywhere else, there are always people in search of the ultimate tool that will trace all relationships and make a difficult reality seem rapidly comprehensible.

This is the reason why simple models that do not really explain much have had such a disproportionate impact. If there were more training in strategic leadership, leading businessmen would be more inclined to make the mental effort to grasp all the interconnected relationships of business management and would therefore be more realistic in their expectation of the capabilities of such tools.

We must remember that training in strategic leadership is still in the embryo stage and does not exist anywhere in fully fledged form. One way to learn is to read books on the subject by good authors. Another is to train oneself to use analytic perception, creativity and experience to work out strategies for different situations.

The experience component in strategy training is of fundamental importance. This is why it is difficult to teach strategy to your university and college students: to be able to apply what they are taught, they must first be able to appreciate the realities of business management. Strategy training can therefore most suitably be given to individuals who have advanced some way in their companies and have had time to accumulate some experience.

The author who has gone farthest in describing typical situations and case histories is Michael Porter, who has compiled a collection of case histories in his book *Competitive Strategy*.

In this chapter I shall deal with some of the definitions and concepts in the field of strategy development that are known by experience to be difficult.

First, under the heading of 'concepts of the strategic process', I shall analyse some central concepts like corporate mission, goal and strategy. In conjunction with this I shall also explain some intermediate forms which occur in discussions of strategy and which are sometimes very valuable in strategy work, depending on type of business and corporate structure.

The section headed 'business structure' deals with the various constellations of people for whom strategies need to be developed and goals set. These concepts will be used in the following two chapters, which deal with the process of strategy.

The section on the elements of strategy is a model that I often use to make strategy operative and concrete. One of the definitions of the concept of strategy refers specifically to the deployment of corporate resources as an overriding expression of strategic orientation; the purpose of the elements of strategy is to depict resource deployment in the broad sense and the direction in which it steers the company.

Concepts of the strategic process

There are three central terms that have special significance in strategy development processes. They are *corporate mission*, *goal* and *strategy*. To avoid lengthy terminological debate, these terms need to have their meanings defined and their relationships to each other and to other terms explained.

Figure 3 gives brief definitions of the three basic terms.

Fig. 3 The three basic concepts of the strategic process

CORPORATE MISSION	An opportunity to do business by supplying a product that is in demand.
	A corporate mission is defined by:
	* needs
	* product
	* customers/market
	* competitors.
GOAL	A term used of various phenomena described in the text, principally:
	* the owner's or leader's *vision*
	* the management's *level of ambition*
	* qualitative and quantitative *goals*.
STRATEGY	An integrated pattern of actions designed to reach specified goals.
	A method of concentrating a company's resources into those areas which offer the best prospects for long-term growth, stable profitability and competitive edge.

Corporate mission

The phenomenon described by the term 'corporate mission' (or sometimes 'business concept') is of Scandinavian origin and may not be so familiar elsewhere. There are two great advanatages to talking about a company's corporate mission: one is that it provides a useful expression of a company's *Raison d'être* that can be communicated to customers and employees, and the other is that the discussion, which concerns the true business essence of the company's operations, is usually of great value in clarifying the company's position.

It is often maintained that a corporate mission should be unique: the more exclusive the corporate mission, the easier it must be to run a profitable operation. In my own opinion, the criterion of exclusiveness is overrated. I have seen examples of splendidly successful companies whose corporate missions differed very little from their competitors'. Strategy formulation and drive are such important components of success that exclusiveness by itself is far from decisive. Naturally, however, the more exclusive the corporate mission, the easier it is to set up and operate the business.

Discussion of the corporate mission concept has also tended to become somewhat academic. There is a school of thought which holds that the corporate mission should be extended to include the company's organization, system of controls, etc. The most practical way to use the term, however, is to express it in the quantities used for a business unit.

The corporate mission satisfies:

(a)   a *need*
(b)   experienced by certain *customers*
(c)   by supplying a *product* comprising an assortment of goods and/or services
(d)   in an *industry* with a number of known *competitors*.

Defined this way, a corporate mission is practically the same thing as an opportunity for earning money in a market of a given structure. But the corporate mission remains no more than an idea unless somebody designs a product and sets up an organization to satisfy the need on which the corporate mission is based.

In business structures the corporate mission concept is used to designate and define a business unit. And a business unit is the central concept for which a business strategy must be devised. As we shall see in the next section, a business unit in its turn can be divided into segments and niches.

One of the more fruitful consequences of corporate mission discussions is that they provide a check that the product really matches the need and the demand. As companies grow, the emphasis tends to shift from the market and the needs of customers to more internal considerations like production facilities, personnel, and often internal communications. When market demand gradually changes in the meantime, the company is often too slow in making the corresponding changes in its product. If this happens, the company starts running into 'sales resistance', which leads to falling profits and, at worst, to production being cut back and employees laid off.

27

A discussion of corporate mission can often have an enormously salutary effect by highlighting the match or mismatch between product on the one hand and need and demand on the other. The term 'product' is used here as a generic word for goods and services. There is a tendency, particularly in high-technology manufacturing industries, to underestimate the importance of the product's service component in customers' choice of suppliers.

SAS Cargo identified the following business structure in its corporate mission:

> The *needs* varied somewhat in nature. In the case of regular flows of goods the prime need was to minimize the amount of capital tied up in stocks – at the factory, in transit and in depots near the customers. The other need was referred to as emergency freight – items that had to be moved quickly in breakdown situations.
>
> The *product* consisted in essence of fast transportation – in SAS's case mostly by air. Initially the product was defective in terms of speed and precision, but these defects were remedied.
>
> The *market* was defined as Scandinavia, which implied that traffic from the European mainland to foreign destinations was not of primary interest. The emphasis was on Scandinavian business and customers who wanted goods flown to or from Scandinavia.
>
> The *competition* in the intercontinental market consisted first and foremost of major European airlines like Lufthansa and British Airways. Within Europe the chief competitors were road haulage firms operating with a high degree of precision.

The corporate mission, based on an analysis of these components, was accordingly defined and expressed as follows:

> On the basis of the needs of Scandinavian business SAS Cargo will contribute to a reduction in tied-up capital and will provide quick and accurate transportation of urgent emergency supplies.

While we are on the subject, we may note that a gradual but dramatic change is now taking place in the transportation business because the relative share of transport costs in the price of goods is falling, while the capital cost component is rising. This shift offers scope for new ideas, as well as for changes in the vertical structure of the industry. In this way a discussion of corporate mission can make a real contribution to promoting the habit of strategic thinking in business.

One important aspect is the obvious fact that corporate missions age like any other ideology. Just as politics is no longer a contest between Whigs and Tories, so there is no longer a demand for horse-drawn vehicles. The underlying needs are undoubtedly still the same, but entirely new ways of satisfying those needs have created totally different demands. The need for transportation is constant, but cars satisfy that need better than horses and buggies.

The evolution of the consumer cooperative movement provides an illustrative example. There was a very distinct need for consumer cooperatives 75–100 years ago. The circumstances that gave them a very strong ideological ground to stand on have gradually changed, and this has led to a need for reorientation and a new ideal.

Intelligent reflection on the ideological position and evolution of your own industry and your own corporate mission can be a very rewarding exercise.

Goals of various kinds

The term 'goal' is actually used here to refer to a number of different expressions of *'the height of the bar'*.

Vision is normally used to refer to a conception of a relatively distant future in which the business has developed under the most favourable conditions exactly according to the owner's or chief executive's hopes and dreams. A vision provides a benchmark for business ambitions upon which the level of ambition of the strategy programme can be dimensioned.

Vision has come to play a growing part in the context of modern corporate change. The term is intimately associated with entrepreneurial behaviour and a high level of ambition, which is one of the reasons why it has become so important. One of the purposes of vision is to create a yardstick of future goals achievement against which present performance can be measured. Vision, moreover, is much less precise than other criteria for designing corporate goals. A vision need not necessarily be realised, but can and should be revised in the light of results to date. This is now Hickman and Silva (1984) describe a vision:

Essentially, vision is a mental journey from the known to the unknown, creating the future from a montage of current facts, hopes, dreams, dangers and opportunities.'

Vision can be said to link business with corporate culture, creating a common norm for evaluation of the performance of individual employees.

Level of ambition is the performance motivation that impels the chief executive or top-management when they decide what the strategy programme is required to accomplish. One of the commonest sources of conflict within managements is that levels of ambition are out of phase, for example between the head of a business unit and his superiors. I know of cases where a keen chief executive has obviously set performance goals on the basis of his own level of ambition, but omitted to secure acceptance of those goals by the people responsible for reaching them. Dissatisfaction from above and frustration from beneath are common reactions in such cases.

Goal is used here both as a generic term and as a designation for the concrete results of visions and levels of ambition, and for the benchmarks against which the eventual success of strategy programmes are to be judged. Goals should perhaps be expressed in the first instance as levels of performance to be achieved in dealings with customers. Goals expressed in this way are more likely to appeal to people in the organization than are abstract expressions of profitability such as return on equity. Goals, then, should be expressed in whatever terms are best calculated to involve people and arouse their enthusiasm.

The object of clearly stating visions, levels of ambition and goals is to raise the level of performance of the organization by involving people in more meaningful activity.

There is nothing manipulative in this definition: it simply states the elementary fact that it feels more meaningful to work in an organization with goals than in one without them.

Strategy

'Strategy' is a term that is often fuzzily defined. There are innumerable definitions, all the way from from the structured long-term horizon of the planning epoch to more diffuse variants of a general nature. I have chosen to define strategy as a means of reaching goals.

To put it more precisely, we can say that strategy is an integrated pattern of actions designed to reach specified goals. The actions are integrated in that they affect several interacting functions of departments. Important questions in connection with the strategy process are where are we going, what shall we do, how shall we do it, and why.

The term *strategy development* is generally applied to the

whole process of formulating a rigorous corporate mission, establishing goals, and devising strategies at portfolio, business unit and functional (departmental) level.

✓ The purpose of strategy is to achieve a permanent competitive edge that gives good profitability. Strategy consists of an integrated pattern of actions designed to reach specified goals by steering and coordinating the company's resources.

The strategy development process is the whole process that comprises definition of corporate mission, concretization of vision, determination of level of ambition, and formulation and implementation of strategies to achieve the stated goals.

One of the great arts in strategy development is that of translating strategic thinking into concrete action and achieving a high factor in implementation. Chapters 3 and 4 deal with the whole of the strategy development process as defined here.

Business structure

This section will deal with the answer to the question 'strategies for what?' I have found by practical experience that one of the most effective ways to start a process of change and development is to use the structures described here to determine the business structure of a company.

Practically all companies comprise more than one business unit and thus constitute a portfolio. A prime requirement for high efficiency in strategy development is a correct definition of the portfolio and its component business units. The difference between portfolio strategy and business strategy can be defined as follows:

BUSINESS STRATEGY	Finding ways to compete effectively and achieve a more favourable position for *one* business unit in *one* industry with *one* group of competitors.
PORTFOLIO STRATEGY	Controlling a portfolio of *different* business units belonging to *different* industries competing under *different* conditions.

Reality is less neatly compartmentalized than this normative classification might lead you to suppose. Business is full of 'synergistic portfolios' – hybrids between portfolios and business units. A company can well supply the customers with different but related products to satisfy different but related needs. In data consultancy, for example, you might find a business unit that supplies its customers needs for both personal and mainframe computers. There are considerable synergies in needs, customers and production, and the division between business units is far from sharp. The same thing applies to travel agencies who serve both business travellers and tourists, and to builders who build both houses and apartment blocks. The division into business units should be contolled by the nature of the market and the behaviour of competitors rather than according to internally established criteria.

Business strategy is sometimes called *competitive strategy,* which is rather confusing. In this discussion I have chosen to use the term 'business strategy' because it relates to the terms business unit and corporate mission, about which I shall have more to say later on.

There are actually only three 'pure' kinds of organizational units for which goals must be set and strategies formulated. They are described in Fig. 4.

Fig. 4 Definitions of organizational units

PORTFOLIO	Consists of a number of business units under common ownership; the points of contact between them may be few or many.
BUSINESS UNIT	The unit for which a business strategy must be formulated; a business unit is defined by * product * needs * customers * competitors.
FUNCTIONS	The specialized departments or other subdivisions of a business unit by virtue of whose combined efforts the business unit does business; examples are marketing, production, R&D, personnel, information systems (EDP), and design.

Portfolio

If you are managing a portfolio, this means in the extreme case that you are constantly concerned with business structures; in fact you are probably the head of a conglomerate group of companies in the 'business unit' industry or, as an approximation, possibly in corporate management (a corporation often consists of several business units). It is your business to:

- buy your way into new industries;
- reinforce existing business units by acquisition;
- pull out of unwanted industries;
- sell off business units that could find more favourable structures elsewhere;
- allocate resources in the form of capital and costs;
- ensure that your business units are strategically managed, and take advantage of synergistic effects between the business units in your portfolio.

The question of portfolio or business unit is often diffuse, giving rise to lengthy discussions, problems of definition and other uncertainties. There is also a boundary zone between managing a portfolio on the one hand and a business unit on the other. I shall return to this point under the next heading, symbiosis in portfolios.

If you are responsible for managing a conglomerate comprising a number of corporate missions that have no strong links with each other, one of your chief problems is probably that of deciding to pull out of structures in which your chances of success are poor. There may after all be other ownership structures that would be much more beneficial to the business units concerned. I have gradually become convinced that you always try to do what is best in the long term for the individual business unit. It is so easy to find reasons not to disinvest. Here are some of them:

- *Power.* You naturally come over as a more important person if you have influence over as much as possible.
- *Prestige.* You want to prove that you can turn the tide in a faltering business unit and win out over the competition.
- *Greed.* You have invested capital in the business unit and want a return on your investment (which, of course, is a matter of total indifference to potential buyers).
- *Sentiment.* Family considerations or personal involvement make it hard to take the decision to disinvest.
- *Habit.* The business has been around so long that you have forgotten why it was acquired in the first place and keep it on as a matter of course.
- *Pride.* We are an expansive corporation and we aren't about to sell anything.

33

This list makes no claim to being complete, nor are the reasons listed mutually exclusive. A skilled and successful corporate chief executive generally knows by experience that the right structure means better total profitability. So if he can find a potential buyer for a given unit whose prospects for making a success of the operation are better than his own, he has a chance to get a price that reflects the value of the business unit to the buyer rather than its value to the seller.

There are of course better and worse negotiating positions. If for example there is only one natural buyer, and that buyer is aware of the seller's situation, it can be difficult to bring the negotiations to a satisfactory conclusion.

On the other hand, there may be good and convincing grounds for the continued existence and growth of the portfolio. A group of companies that is a conglomerate today may owe its origins to other than purely financial considerations. Here are some good reasons for having a portfolio of different business units:

- Business dynamics have led to organic growth, which has created a more or less synergistic portfolio.
- 'Technology push' (see Chapter 5, p. 128 for an explanation of this term) has led to the development of business areas that are totally unrelated business-wise, but use related technology.
- The business has been so successful that existing operations cannot absorb all the money available for investment, so the money has had to be put into new businesses.
- It has been a deliberate policy to spread risks.
- The combination of business units is strongly synergistic.

The motives for and advantages of having a portfolio are not hard to find. However, experience indicates that portfolios can easily become static to a degree that goes counter to their owners' intentions.

Symbiosis in portfolios

It is not uncommon to find a business portfolio with strong common links in some individual basic respect. It may be that the units are all selling to the same customers, or are developing products from the same chemical raw material, or using the same manufacturing plant. It is important to pay due heed to the organic links that exist and refrain from drawing hard lines of demarcation through the function that constitutes the horizontal link and may be the key to the growth of the whole corporation.

As we shall see in the next section, the business unit concept is defined by what distinguishes one unit from another. But while making such distinctions we must also take careful note of common elements between units.

> Some years ago, practically all the car companies in the Western world reorganized themselves into a divisionalized structure with one division to sell new cars, one to handle service, and maybe a third for spare parts. It has gradually become evident that the needs of many enlightened customers have to do with car ownership as a whole rather than with each of these three functions separately. Not so long ago I met the head of a large American car corportion's Norwegian subsidiary who was fully aware of this but could not do anything about it, being bound by the corporation's international directives.
>
> The symbiosis between the three functions is now obvious to most people, and we can expect to see a shift to a different organizational pattern in the car trade.

I recently encountered a similar situation in another industry, the building trade.

> A medium-sized building company was in process of organizing itself according to what it perceived as being two distinct business areas: construction and real estate. In the present state of the market construction just about breaks even, whereas real estate business can operate at a normal profit. The intention was to split these two types of business up for executive purposes. But on closer investigation it turned out that a strong symbiotic relationship existed butween the two. The real estate business, which seemed to have independent profit-earning capability, would in fact run a serious risk of 'impotence', i.e. of winding up in a situation where real estate was bought and sold without access to the improvement knowhow on which its profit potential was actually based. If one side was dropped, the other would run into difficulties.

Synergies between intrinsically separate business units presents one of the more difficult organizational problems that must be solved in practice. Such relationships exist in nearly all companies. A common mistake is to let synergies on the production side control in a situation that calls for a high degree of market orientation. Another thing that often happens is that organizational integration is based on products without reference to customer needs, which should be the prime consideration.

Errors of synergy.

35

A not too daring hypothesis is that the nature of the most important horizontal links varies with the state of maturity of the industry. In the computer industry today, as in the rock drill industry back in the days when it was new, the technological links were the most important ones. But the rock drill industry has (and the computer industry will) gradually become more and more of a commodity market, in which first product links and later customer links assume greater importance. The design of the organization must of course be based on the relevant horizontal links, but changes in organization are usually slow to follow changes in the relative importance of different links.

This, is one reason why it is so vital that strategists know the historical background of the industries they deal with. Such Such knowledge gives insights into the evolution of the horizontal links, which can often provide the key to successful change.

We do not speak of a corporate mission for a portfolio. But we can very well speak of portfolio goals insofar as a vision exists of how the portfolio should develop and what its future composition should be. We can also envisage portfolio strategies, i.e. integrated patterns of action designed to reach those goals.

I have taken part in many discussions in which attempts have been made to find a corporate mission statement for an entire portfolio. Such statements are invariably so stretched and diluted as to lose all substance, so exercises of this kind seldom accomplish anything worth while. The discussion ought to concentrate instead on how the structure of the portfolio needs to be changed and what one wants to gain by doing so. It is quite possible to generate strategic hypotheses for a portfolio in the usual way, as will be described in the next chapter.

In addition to changes in the structure of the portfolio, a group management should also survey the relationships between its business units and try to use those relationships to win a competitive edge for the whole portfolio. As in the case of business strategy this can be done within individual departments – production, distribution, sales, etc. A group of companies should work out a conscious portfolio strategy aiming at a systematic search for mechanisms for identifying relationships and taking advantage of them. This is sometimes called horizontal strategy.

Business units operating independently of each other are seldom motivated to propose strategies based on portfolio links. The heads of business portfolios have a broader purview, and it is their responsibility to optimize the whole by utilizing whatever horizontal advantages they can find. It is possible, without disrupting the organizational structure, to set up special committees or task forces – not to be confused with a matrix organization – for the purpose. There might for example be one group to study dealer technology, another to study links on the production side, and so on.

The term 'strategic sector' refers here to parts of a portfolio or complete companies which, while they ought to have their own individual strategies, also exhibit a strong organic relationship in the form of a basic function from which the different business units derive. An example of such a function is the chemical engineering sector in a group of companies manufacturing both toothpaste and scouring powder. These products bear no relation whatsoever to each other in terms of consumer needs, but they do have a synergistic relationship in the distribution phase, and possibly also in the manufacturing phase.

Another example of a strategic sector is the data consultancy industry, which from a common technological base develops different products to satisfy different needs, sometimes for the same users and sometimes for different ones.

The important need is to develop one strategy for the common denominator in a strategic sector.

> Never forget the cost of coordination, compromise and loss of flexibility often outweighs the apparent economies of scale gained by pooling resources. What looks like a more rational set-up may not in fact be more efficient.

Business unit

The business unit is the fundamental particle for which a *business strategy* must be formulated. A business unit operates with a specific corporate mission in a specific industry and is characterized by:

- a distinctive *product* comprising goods and/or services
- which satisfy the specified *needs*
- of a group of *customers*
- in a certain market, i.e. one with certain specific *competitors*.

This definition of a business unit implies that we single out a certain part of our business and say that this is a business unit, while at the same time considering factors and functions that unite this particular business unit with the rest of our business.

An *industry* is the sum of all business units within a given area of need. Thus the term has nothing to do with the legal constitution of a company. The reason why I have chosen to deal with industries after business units is that the determintion of a strategy for a business unit ought always to involve a competition analysis of the part of the industry that operates in or near one's own market. Thus an American building company would probably not need to analyse the building industry in New Zealand. See also the section on industries and markets on p. 43 ff.

Figure 5 shows the most important relationships for a business unit. One can of course have a vision and a level of ambition concerning a portfolio, and ideas about the composition and development of that portfolio. It is however wrong to try and formulate a corporate mission that covers a whole portfolio, because the result will be so vague as to be meaningless. Instead you should try to develop strategies around the horizontal links or symbiotic relationships that exist within the framework of a business portfolio.

Fig. 5 *Strategy relationships for a business unit*

As we have seen, there is often some relationship between the business units in a portfolio. And as mentioned above, we can use the term 'strategic sector' for a group of business units with a clearly defined interrelationship.

A *segment* is a group of buyers with common needs which can be satisfied by a product that distinguishes itself in some

38

respect from what is being sold on the total market. 'Segment' is thus a designation referring to a group of customers in a total market who have special needs as a common characteristic. A segment is a subset of the market concept, which is one of the determining parameters of the business unit. The reason why the term is defined here is that segmentation is often used as a basis for the organization of a business unit. The distinction between market and segment is not hard and fast, but is rather a question of which total set is used as a basis for talking about segments. Take cars, for example. The market set can be said to consist of small cars, light cars, medium cars and large cars. But the subset of medium cars can also be segmented into standard family cars, low-price cars, and special cars like BMW and Volvo. The special category can be divided still further, and so on.

There is really only one factor that makes a particular subset of a total market set a segment, and that is the structure of customer needs. When we read about segmentation, we often find that it is based on a variety of criteria: geography, demography, age, buying habits, etc. On closer consideration we find tht all these criteria are simply approximations to one criterion: need. I have seen examples of attempts at segmentation which were *less* successful because they were made on a basis of statistical groupings instead of need.

A travel agency classified its customers according to a number of criteria including age and purpose of journey. It then tried to differentiate its product on the basis of this classification. The attempt was not a success because travellers did not in fact make any correlation between their choice of carrier and the purpose of their journey.

Identifying the true structure of needs is something of an art form, so segmentation is a point that needs special attention, preferably with creative people on the team assigned to it.

The business unit is the central concept in strategy development, even in groups of companies. A group or portfolio is no more than the sum of its component business units unless there are synergetic factors present, relationships that operate to the mutual benefit of the business units. Herein lies the difference between a *diversified conglomerate*, in which such relationships are lacking, and an *organic portfolio*, where a clear relationship exists. Necessarily, then, the goals of a diversified conglomerate will lie more in the area of financial management and profit maximization, while the primary goals of business units and portfolios with an organic make-up will consist primarily of the dominating leaders' visions, with qualitative goals of various kinds in second place, and translations of these into quantitative and market-related goals maybe only in third place.

A *niche* is a segment of the kind described above in which the competitive pressure is less intense than in the market as a whole. 'Niche', too, is a much used an much abused word, but nevertheless a very useful one when we want to characterize and focus upon a given target group in a total market set. Consider for example the building of ambulances by a large passenger car manufacturer. Most of the major automotive companies have no interest in ambulance at all; in Europe it is only Mercedes and Volvo who have made a speciality of that particular kind of vehicle. To relatively small companies like those two, such a niche can be very interesting indeed.

Functional strategies

Functions are the various component activities – usually assigned to specialist departments in the organizational structure – that go to make up a business unit. All the functions must be directed in accordance with the business strategy in order to make the strategy work efficiently. It is the various functions of the business unit that must translate abstract strategic thinking into plans and programmes.

It is not unusual to find some functions trailing behind in the process of strategy development. The farther from profit-centre responsibility a given function is located, the harder it is for the strategies to influence its work. Functions like EDP (electronic data processing) or personnel can be difficult to influence. In the EDP field, moreover, there is a great shortage of qualified personnel, and this does not help to motivate a change in behaviour patterns.

Heads of departments have a tendency to claim that their function is so vitally important to the company's operations that it must be handled at top management level. We have all heard such claims from public relations, personnel, computer section and other managers.

These claims are correct insofar as functional strategies undoubtedly are an essential issue for the attention of top management. If a new hiring policy is to be adopted or a new computer system purchased, the decision is naturally one of central and strategic importance. However, the claims are *not* true to the extent that all departmental issues always demand the undivided attention of top management.

One can for example trace the rise and fall in the importance of different corporate functions at different times. The marketing function is a good example of a function that swiftly rose in importance with the growth of sales resistance in the 1960s. Similarly, since the end of the 1970s the administration of capital has become more important than ever before as managements have realized the need for careful management of capital resources in a high-interest climate.

We can probably now look forward to a period of ascendancy for the personnel function, albeit in a new role. Employee motivation and business efficiency will probably become more and more important as competitive weapons, and this will affect the way personnel departments operate. The same applies to the purchasing function.

It is usually much easier to bring about a strategic re-orientation of functions like marketing that are directly exposed to competition. In connection with strategic change a 'marketing audit' can be an effective tool for rethinking in the marketing function. A marketing audit involves a critical scrutiny of the efficiency of marketing, using a zero-based approach (totally disregarding how marketing is actually run) to reconstruct an input of marketing measures that is quite independent of the current allocation of resources. One technique that can be used in this context is to measure market penetration by the awareness/trial order/repeat order model illustrated in Fig. 6. This technique provides information about the efficiency of the marketing function and about the quality of the product, i.e. how well it matches customers' needs.

Thus if we decide on a principal strategy, e.g. 'businessman's airline', the marketing function must of course, like every other function, be geared to support the chosen strategy. It must in other words have its own functional (departmental) strategy.

Functional companies actually represent a special case of functional strategy, though the situation here is often more complicated. In the first place you have an autonomous management with its own chief executive who may have his own ambitions in the way of business development, and in the second place you often have the problem that there are

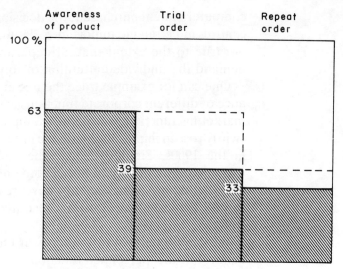

Fig. 6 Test of efficiency of marketing

several business units integrated into one company. Certain problems of transition always arise when the results of strategic planning at business strategy level have to be broken down and applied at functional company level. You should begin by establishing what degree of strategic autonomy the functional unit can be allowed; this increases your chances of getting the results you want.

The term *market strategy* is used in two senses. In the first sense it is synonymous with the concept of competitive strategy, or even sometimes of business strategy, but with the restriction that it then generally refers to methods of competition in certain given circumstances, e.g. with a given production apparatus or with a given frame of resources in terms of costs and investment. In the second sense it is synonymous with marketing strategy or the functional strategy for the company's marketing department.

The hierarchy of strategy

The hierarchy of strategy is such that the strategy of one level becomes the goal of the level below it. If one loses sight of this fact, the discussions can become extremely confused. The phenomenon is illustrated in Fig. 7. Portfolio strategies, devised with a view to reaching portfolio goals, guide the setting of goals for subsidiaries or business units. To reach these goals the business units must have their own strategies, which in turn translate into goals for their various functions. Conversely, the goal of one level becomes the strategy of the level above it. The next two chapters deal with how goals are set and strategies worked out.

Fig. 7 The hierarchy of strategy

PORTFOLIO	*Goal:*	Risk spreading with the emphasis on high risk/high return, rapid expansion and concentration on electronic industries. 20% in R_T, 35% in R_E
	Strategy:	Increase market shares in production of services.
SERVICE PRODUCING BUSINESS UNIT	*Goal:*	Increase market share of data consultancy by 20%
	Strategy:	Reinforce sales function and boost sales.
SALES FUNCTION	*Goal:*	Increase number of salespeople to 8, increase sales volume by 4800 man-hours.
	Strategy:	Try to poach competitors' best salespeople, reinforce sales management.

The arena of strategy – industry and market

The term 'industry' in the context of this book was defined earlier as the sum of all the business units operating in a given area of need. This may not be quite the whole truth, as the geographical aspect is also highly relevant to the definition of an industry.

One of the pitfalls of strategy lies in defining your market as coterminous with the market you are actually supplying. That way you miss the competitive pressure emanating from the operations of competitors outside the market you are supplying.

British Ferranti, for example, can define its market for electronic components as the United Kingdom. The company may have a large market share in the UK while simultaneously operating on the edge of bankruptcy, because the market is in fact global and companies like Texas Instruments, thanks to economics of scale, are generating much larger returns.

The globalization of industries is one of the most salient features of the contemporary business scene, and must be taken into account. A striking illustration is provided by what is now happening in the automotive industry. The Japanese recognized the need for globalization and identified components as the most important cost item for cars in the mass-market segment. The key to competitive success, then, lay in minimizing the number of components, standardizing them so that they could be used in different models, and designing cars that would sell in many countries, thereby achieving low unit production costs. In this way the Japanese have won huge cost advantages, being able to produce a typical light car for an estimated 1000 – 2000 dollars less than their European and American competitors.

Automotive companies that had not already globalized their operations have now been forced to think again. Austin Rover (formerly British Leyland), for example, has begun to collaborate with Honda, and Alfa-Romeo in Italy with Nissan, while Renault in France is trying to globalize itself by teaming up with American manufacturers, particularly American Motors (now terminated).

The example of the automotive industry illustrates the danger of equating the market with that part of it one is currently supplying. Whoever takes the initiative to globalization generally gains the advantage and forces his competitors to retreat.

The telecommunications industry offers another example. Companies that have confined themselves to seemingly large enough domestic markets, like CGE in France and Plessey in Britain, have experienced serious difficulties, while others like AT&T, Northern Telecom, Siemens and Ericsson internationalized their operations long ago and now look likely to emerge as the winners from the restucturing process that is going on in the industry. ITT is a special case in that it has given up its efforts to adapt its system to its home market (the United States), and now seems to be in process of retiring from active competition in the field of telecommunications. Developments in the next few years will certainly show some prime examples of restructuring and globalization.

In fact it is no exaggeration to say that the worst possible thing to do in an industry that is going global is to stay at home and just compete in one's own market. A company that only operates in its home market will miss out on the fast-growing markets in the rest of the world, and will see

44

more enterprising competitiors utilizing their growth to gain the advantages of scale and undermining the profitability of the stay-at-home company's operations on its own domestic market. It will find itself under attack on its home ground from other companies armed with superior technology, design, manufacturing and marketing.

That is why it is vital to see the direction in which your industry is moving and recognize when it is in the process of globalization of internationalization. The direction and speed of the current trend are key factors. Another is the realization that you can influence the course of events in the industry by taking the initiative yourself.

In an internationalized industry it is necessary to develop strategies for internationalization while clearly understanding the need to have local market strategies for each national or regional market. The structure of market needs varies from one country to another, and it is important not to lose sight of this fact in discussions of international strategies, which often have to do with some aspect of the economics of scale. Globalization further involves acquiring international skills and reshaping corporate cultures. A globalization effort unaccompanied by changes in management style, corporate culture and accumulation of know-how has little chance of succeeding.

Finally, let us take a look at the competitive situation between Austin Rover and Ford in the UK as an illustration of the importance of the 'industry' concept relative to market supplied and profitability. In the 1970s, British Leyland (as Austin Rover was then called) defined the market it was supplying as the British market, and its share of that market was larger than Ford's. The classic strategic dictum that a large market share means large profits did not hold good in the UK : British Leyland recorded heavy losses, while Ford enjoyed a normal return on its capital.

Strategic groups

As a final point in discussing the arena of strategy I would like to take up the question of strategic groups – a point which has been admirably covered by Porter, for example, in his book *Competitive Strategy*. Strategic groups 'are groups of companies in the same industry with characteristics that make them similar to each other but different from other groups of companies in that industry'. The division into strategic groups is often made on the basis of one variable that constitutes a key strategic factor in the industry concerned. The packaging industry, for example, could be grouped according to whether companies base their strategies on the economics of scale or on a differentiated product with a high value-added component. The building trade could be grouped according to whether companies concentrate on building private houses, apartment houses, commercial buildings or industrial plants.

A choice of strategy can often be a matter of deliberately moving from one strategic group to another. You can for example opt to switch from making an undifferentiated standard product to making a highly differentiated product aimed at a special segment of the market. The history of the Saab-Scania Car Division is a case in point: with the launch of the Saab 9000 Turbo 16 model, Saab has taken a definitive step out of the ordinary special vehicle segment, where many of the world's automative companies are active, into a more exclusive segment of which BMW is a typical representative.

A division into strategic groups can be a great help in discussions of trends in an industry and how to position your own company in that industry.

The elements of strategy

In conjunction with strategy development processes I have experienced a strong need to concentrate strategic thinking with reference to the implementation process. For this purpose I found it useful to specify a number of key variables that control the way a company or business unit deploys its resources. I call these variables the *elements of strategy*.

The elements of strategy can also be used to analyse and determine what strategy a company actually has. If you survey the nine elements of strategy in a compnay (Fig. 8), you can arrive at a very good appreciation of just how consciously it is following a strategic course.

> The elements of strategy comprise a number of partly overlapping factors that make a business strategy operational.

These elements taken together provide an excellent indicator of how a company or business unit is using and marshalling its resources to move in a given direction.

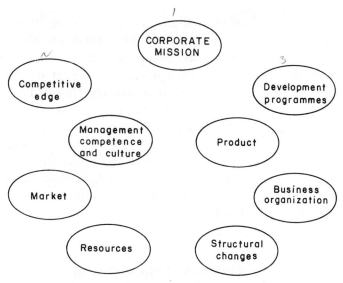

Fig. 8 The elements of strategy

Corporate mission

The concept of corporate mission represents the opportunity that exists on a market to satisy defined *needs* by supplying a given *product* to a given category of *customers* in competition with a given group of *competitors*. As I pointed out earlier, corporate missions have a tendency to age, which often gives rise to uncertainty as to means of competition and product.

It is usually fairly easy to tell how clear a strategy is by noting how the management of a company defines its corporate mission. There is a tendency to stagnate in old, well-worn patterns when it comes to reinterpreting the needs that lie behind the demand one meets and tracing changes in the structure of need over a period of time. Demand is subject to constantly changing influences, e.g. from new products and new technology developed by competitors. The underlying needs are usually fairly constant, while demand shifts towards the product that best satisfies those needs.

Competitive edge

Perhaps the most important element of strategy is the choice of how to compete. The purpose of the strategy can be expressed as achieving a higher degree of need satisfaction than the competition can achieve, and thereby gaining a position that will generate a rate of profit above the average for the industry. The aim of securing a competitive edge is intimately associated with the choice of markets and ajustments of the product, for example, but it can also effect the structure of investments. If you choose a strategy for efficiency in production and cost advantage, this may mainly affect production structures, investment, and development projects concerned with the economics of production. In mass markets with few opportunities for product differentiation, the competitive edge chosen will not be the same as in, say, a service market where the possibilities for varying the product are wider.

Business organization

Business organization refers to the way an organization subdivides itself for business purposes. Almost every company has an organization that is differentiated on the basis of business in the form of products, product groups, customers or markets. Part of the company's strategy is reflected in how its business organization is first differentiated and then integrated. If for example you are selling Renault products in Canada and Norway, you will probably differentiate the business *vis-à-vis* the market into trucks and cars. You will then integrate the business into a national sales company, which in turn represents a differentiation on the basis of geographical markets. Then you integrate that into a regional organization on the one hand and a product group organization on the other.

Product

'Product' is used here as a generic term for goods and services. It may be difficult to form a complete picture of how well the product matches the structure of customers' needs, but you should make a real effort to do so. One way is to find out whether the company has made any recent attempt to check its product against customers' needs. You can also check up on how much of your turnover comes from *new* products and services, to get an idea of how the total product is evolving. Yet another idea is to consider how a hardware-producing company has built up services to support its hardware.

Markets

Markets are not defined by geography alone, but also by the application or use of the product. You may for example want to select certain segments or a niche in which you think the pressure of competition will be less.

The infinite corporate mission is to sell everything to everybody everywhere. In your strategy development you have to narrow down that limitless vista according to your corporate mission so that you can concentrate your energies on the customers you most want to sell to. This process of defining primary target groups may seem an obvious step, but it is often neglected. In fact it is one of the most essential elements of strategy.

Resources

Resources in this context comprise investments and costs. Investments are usually channelled to support the strategy, and their nature says a lot about a company's dominant value judgements and strategies. In the of an airline, for example, you can note whether it has put most of its investment into buying new aircraft or into upgrading its personnel and range of services. If you find a shipping company that has invested in real estate over a long period of time, that says something about is strategies in just the same way as if it had invested heavily in new ships. Development of markets, personnel and other software can also be regarded as investments. The orientation of the whole cost complex is a decisive element of strategy.

Structural changes

Structural changes, or the buying and selling of companies and business units, are also significant indicators of a company's strategic philosophy. Initiatives for structural change are seldom taken at the business unit level. It is particularly unusual for the head of a business unit to suggest that his unit should be sold to another group of owners. The reason is probably that any such suggestion would be ill received by the present owners. Structural changes naturally give strong clues about a company's view of its own future.

Development programmes

Development of products, markets, business, etc. is usually a part of the total investment programme. Corporate R&D projects are, hopefully, the result of a strategic policy, whether prompted by 'technology push' (see p. 128 ff.) or by market demand. Unfortunately it is not uncommon for a technological culture to acquire its own momentum and engage in development projects unrelated to business strategy. Development programmes are one of the clearest strategic indicators.

Management competence and culture

Management competence and culture are also strategic indicators. You should study how management operates, and especially to what extent entrepreneurship and drive are rewarded or penalized. The level of ambition is usually determined by top management, and it is a good idea to find out whether there is a level of ambition agreed on by all the leading executives, or whether the subject has ever been discussed at all. The degree of strategic leadership ability is naturally just as important. The company's corporate mission, goals and strategies are interesting questions to raise. It is easy to judge the level of strategic leadership ability from the answers; that level may be high, even if the answers do not trip freely off the tongue.

The concept of corporate culture includes a number of basic value judgements that are expressed in various ways. Some of them are:

- the attitude to risk-taking in business;
- acceptance of the entrepreneurial spirit, i.e. high performance motivation and low relation orientation;
- atitudes to quality and customer satisfaction;
- attitudes to people, customers and employees; and
- attitudes to work, success and failure.

Business strategy hybrids

I would like to take up another question of strategic structure connected with an emergent phenomenon in the mixed economy society. It can be interesting to study the elements

50

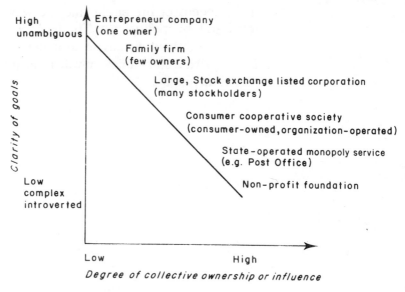

Fig. 9 *Collective influence versus clarity of goals*

of strategy, or how strategy is expressed, in the light of the growing complexity of corporate structures and ownership.

Figure 9 makes no claim to be complete or rigorously correct, but it does illustrate how business organizations of various kinds can be plotted on a coordinate system with the degree of collective influence on one axis and the clarity of their goals on the other. My experience as a consultant indicates that a correlation of the kind illustrated does exist. A significant part of the explanation may be that many collectively owned or public-sector business organizations date back to an earlier period in the evolution of our society. This can in turn explain why their goals have gradually become less well defined, while collective influence continues to carry these organizations forward into a changing world without any strategic reappraisal being made.

The influence of political, trade union, cooperative and other mass movements is so strongl today in many companies and organizations – especially in Scandinavia – that it is important to consider how this factor affects their strategic freedom.

The situation in the public sector is greatly complicated by the fact that the customers' needs are interpreted by others, namely politicians, who strongly influence the shape of the product. Discrepancies are bound to arise between the tangible needs of the public and the way those needs are interpreted by politicians. These discrepancies make it much more difficult to devise strategies for public services than for private companies, in which clarity of goals is much easier to arrive at.

3 The strategic process – vision, understanding the business and analysis

Background and definition

The strategic process embodies the work involved in:

1. defining vision, level of ambition and goals for a business, portfolio or business unit;
2. understanding the trade logic of the industry and the company's business structure;
3. making the necessary analyses of the business environment, the industry and the company;
4. using those analyses to formulate strategies and secure a strategic advantage; and
5. energetically implementing the strategies in such a way as to strengthen the competitive power of the portfolio or business unit and to improve its profitability.

Figure 10 illustrates the structure of the strategy development process which I shall describe in this and the following chapters. This structure has proved very effective, as it includes all the steps that must be taken to reach the goal of the strategic process, viz, a better competitive position and better profitability.

A new model for strategy development

I shall now describe a model for strategy development as illustrated in Fig. 10. There are two requirements for an effective strategy development process: firstly a sequence of steps that naturally follow from and partly overlap each

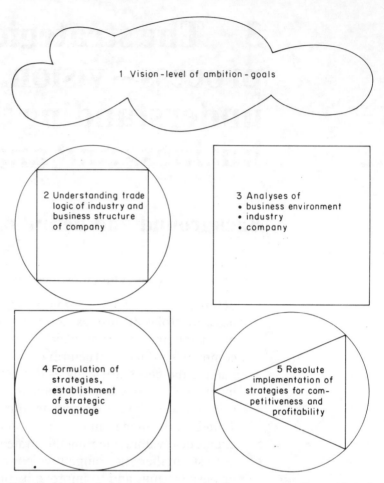

1 Vision - level of ambition - goals

2 Understanding trade
logic of industry and
business structure
of company

3 Analyses of
• business environment
• industry
• company

4 Formulation of
strategies,
establishment
of strategic
advantage

5 Resolute
implementation of
strategies for com-
petitiveness and
profitability

Fig. 10 Model of the strategic process. Squares symbolize analytical components, circles stand for creative components and the triangle represents the dynamic component in the actual implementation.

other, and secondly a common vision, a level of ambition for the strategy development process itself that is accepted by management. Insofar as consultants take part in the process, there must be agreement between them and their clients concerning the level of ambition and the desired degree of efficiency of the strategic process. It takes three things to make the process successful: thought, feeling and action. By this I mean that it calls for both high-level intellectual exertion, a far-reaching commitment on the part of the people responsible for managing the strategy development process and, finally, a high degree of resolution and dynamism in its execution.

The history of corporate strategy is a short one, and the pace of development has been breathtaking. Only ten years

54

ago, operations research techniques were being used largely for the purpose of achieving rational production based on economies of scale. An excellent illustation of how quickly attitudes have changed is to be found in the MIT report on the automotive industry that was published in 1973. It predicted that the number of car manufacturers in the world would shrink to between five and seven; poor odds were given on the survival prospects of smaller companies like BMW and Volvo because their unit costs would be too high.

This report had an enormous impact on the automotive industry. The multinational giants began to design 'world cars' for the sole purpose of making their production rational enough and the economies of scale big enough to enable them to survive the coming structural shake-out.

I cite this example not as a smug expression of hindsight, but first and foremost to emphasize how quickly attitudes to the strategic process have changed. By doing so I want to underline the need to find processes that take account of demands for real, businesslike improvements. It was not so long ago that low unit costs were a guiding principle of practically all strategic thinking. This has come to be somewhat maliciously referred to as the 'McNamara syndrome', alluding to the attitude that characterized Robert McNamara's period as Chief Executive of Ford.

People's desire for individuality, the buyer's desire for a multitude of products to choose from and the product differentiation prompted by these desires have since been recognised as powerful factors underlying product changes.

Volvo and BMW are two examples of companies that have improved their positions by deepening and strengthening their own special segment of the market. I referred in an earlier chapter to Say's law:

Supply creates demand.

This law describes a situation in which a certain need exists, but the demand cannot be qualified because no product exists to satisfy it. Possibilities for product differentiation leading to vitalization of revenues are part of the new-found experience of modern strategy development.

> The danger of models is that they can be too confining – that they can lead to ossification of thought instead of flexibility and creativity. Models, after all, are supposed to be abstractions from reality that can be readily applied to new concrete cases.

Models can be of some help in analysing problems and making decisions without fouling things up. That was one of the guiding principles when the strategy development process described here was worked out. It will hopefully be illustrative, concise, applicable to concrete cases and conducive to consistency in following the process through – which is essential to the efficient development of strategies.

In many organizations a state of tension exists between the present situation and the situation that many dominant individuals consider desirable. This is sometimes called 'structured tension', and is a situation one occasionally encounters in practical strategy work. In such cases it is essential to have strong, progressive executives in the organization who are not just 'parlour pioneers' but have the real driving force needed to bring about radical change. The reason why I mention this is that I have sometimes found such a driving force to be absent – a lack which naturally has a profound influence on the results of strategy development.

The previous chapter dealt with a systematic method of structuring the businesses in a business organization. It is important to know the *reason* for developing a strategy and implementing a process. In this chapter we are dealing with the procedure for achieving strategic development, and can therefore assume that the question of strategic structure is already resolved.

Figure 10 outlines the process. It can be regarded as having two main components, one of which can be termed analytical and the other implementation-oriented.

In recent years there has been a strong tendency to reject the analytical component in favour of action and change. In many cases there has been too little analysis, and this has led to strategy development processes which, though they stirred up a lot of dust, have had a decidedly shaky intellectual foundation. On the other hand, analysis must of course be cost-effective; it should be regarded primarily as an auxiliary function in the process.

The analytical component can be divided into three phases:

1. the level of ambition for strategy development;
2. understanding of trade logic and the company's business structure;
3. analysis of business environment, industry and company.

Following these steps one can generate a material, and probably also a number of strategic hypotheses, which will result in a choice or determination of strategy through a process based on experience of strategy and analytic acumen, but perhaps above all on creative thinking. This choice of strategy will in turn be basic to the implementation, the importance of which has been emphasized increasingly in recent years.

The process of strategy is dealt with in five steps, of which the first three can be regarded as belonging to the analytical component and the last two to the implementation-oriented component. The boundaries are however very fluid, and the development process should be iterative. We can form a mental picture of the process as proceeding according to Fig. 11, which illustrates the thinking behind the strategy development process. I have used broken lines to indicate the difference in level between the analysis applied to the business unit/company and that which refers to the whole portfolio or the individual functions in the unit/company.

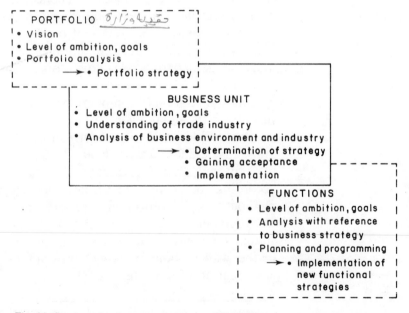

Fig. 11 Strategy development process at different levels: portfolio, business unit and function

Level of ambition – goals

The term 'vision' is sometimes used to signify a more remote conception of the result of business development. Not everybody is a visionary, by any means.

The trouble with visions that are communicated is that they may be viewed as naive and unrealistic pipe-dreams unconnected with workaday realities. The reason may be either that other people lack the visionary's imagination, or that the visionary himself has allowed his imagination to outrun the bounds of feasibility. The dominant individual's conception of the distant future can be valuable in determining how high the strategic sights are set, so visions can and should influence the level of ambition in a company and its strategic work.

The result of the strategy development process depends entirely on the level of ambition of the individuals who *control* the process. These are normally the chief executive and his immediate associates. There are no 'objective' goals, no acknowledged specific results that can or should be achieved in a business operation. Level of ambition is a highly subjective phenomenon, and the establishement of that level and its acceptance by all concerned are among the prime requisites for successful strategy development.

The converse is of course also true, i.e. that lack of concensus on the level of ambition between, say, owners and management or board of directors and management is a sure road to cross-purposes and conflict. I was once involved with a constellation of companies in which a financial result just above the break-even point had long been regarded as an acceptable level of performance. When the owner gradually made harder demands and raised the level of ambition, the individuals who had been behaving according to the old norms naturally began to look like mediocrities or even failures. There are still many heads of companies who are quite content to administer the status quo, having long since given up any ambitions in the way of bold thinking, entrepreneurial risk-taking and creation of new business.

> One of the more dramatic signs of change on the contemporary business scene is the shift from shop-minding to business-developing management.

This shift is often accompanied by the initiation of strategy development processes, and when that happens it is particularly important to atune the ambition levels of all the participants and to set goals of a kind that everyone can agree on. It may sound somewhat childish to harp on the need for compatibility of ambition levels, but experience shows that this cannot be taken for granted. One of the commonest causes of failure, especially when new business ventures are launched in large companies, is the lack of a common level of ambition between top management and the person responsible for leading the new venture.

I have also had occasion to work with clients who made almost impossible demands that their subordinates found exceedingly hard to live up to. Expansion targets were set at totally unrealistic levels. This is the dilemma of the entrepreneur: he often demands levels of performance that are beyond the capabilities of most ordinary mortals.

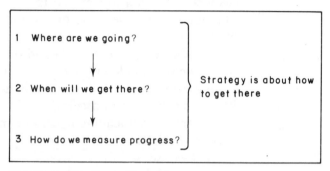

Fig. 12 Outline for setting goals

Trade logic and corporate business structure

An important starting point for understanding trade logic is the value-added component of the industry: how it arises and how it relates to labour and capital. Value added is usually a much more relevant yardstick than, say, turnover, profit, or even return on investment. Not only does value added throw a penetrating light on the workings of industries and the efficiency of companies, but a knowledge of its size and composition can often give useful clues to choice of strategies.

I have already pointed out the complexity of trade logic: at this point I just want to emphasize the lack of insight into logic that is a common side-effect of modern fast career patterns. We have tried to replace the strong empathy that old-time businessmen felt with their own particular lines of business by a more technocratic and much more cerebral, analytical approach. This is not altogether a good thing, because understanding of trade logic is crucial to successful strategy development. Empathy with the industry gives the businessman an extra dimension which, other things being equal, can supply the competitive edge he needs.

The term 'trade logic' refers to the way money is made in an industry, and its complexity can vary widely from one industry to another. Sometimes the logic is fairly easy to explain. Such is often the case in trading companies, where the logic is just as simple as it sounds: selling a commodity at a mark-up that covers the specific costs of the transaction plus a contribution to fixed costs.

In other cases the logic of the industry is much more complex. Communictions equipment for pipelines may for example be needed in Nigeria and bought in Los Angeles after a decision made in London. The respective influences of the parties involved in the decision-making process are diffuse and difficult to ascertain.

Sometimes even leading figures in an industry are ignorant of its logic. They are too preoccupied with the technical aspects to observe how needs are actually structured, and therefore go wrong from the business point of view.

> Analysis of equipment for transporation of small amounts of money from shops to banks or post offices revealed that extensive tests of security bags had been going on since 1910. There had been bags that fired bullets from pistols, bags that released clouds of gas, bags that sprayed dye on the robber and the banknotes, and bags that gave off loud alarm signals. Naturally there were also bags which were simply thief-proof. Trade logic, it seemed, had not been applied at all. The risk of robbery is much greater in the shop itself than on the way to the bank. Weighed against the cost of the bag, the risk did not justify purchase. In addition, a security bag made potential robbery victims easy to identify. Yet experiments with security bags have been going on for 75 years despite the fact that there is no commercial market for them. Not even in Manhattan do messengers carry security bags.

In cases where trade logic is based on symbiosis between different kinds of business it can be particularly difficult to understand how to make money. Airlines, for example, have two main sources of revenue: passengers and cargo The former account for maybe 80% of earnings, the latter for about 20%. The passenger-carrying service is in the nature of a consumer product, whereas the customers for cargo are businesses. Aircraft fleets are dimensioned on a

60

basis of passenger-carrying capacity, while up to 40% of the revenue on intercontinental lines can come from cargo.

If you distribute the capital costs of aircraft on the basis of occupied volume, as is often done, the cargo operation will nearly always show a loss. If you do not understand the logic of the industry you might suggest discontinuing the cargo business (which would cut the profits of an average-sized airline by tens of millions of dollars); or you might suggest having the same sales force for passengers and cargo.

In the goods haulage industry there is a constant struggle in the borderline functions of the vertical integration chain. Forwarding agents want to take over shipper's dispatching functions. Shippers want to integrate forward and take over the functions of forwarding agents. Some companies want to operate their own air or surface freight lines. Forwarding agents want to integrate backward by starting and operating their own road transport and other services. Carriers like airlines try to sell their product direct to shippers. The chaotic state of the freight business is probably an indication that the industry is operating according to an outdated trade logic, and my guess is that new structures are in process of emerging.

A few key questions that may help towards an understanding of trade logic are:

● What needs exist that have to be satisfied?
● What producers exist, and are there different ways of satisfying the needs?
● Who pays for satisfying the needs?
● Is this delivery profitable, or wherein lies profitability?
● How are buyers influenced?

There are few companies in the building industry that show a profit on construction. They make their money out of real estate instead – but they need to be involved in construction in order to be able to make profitable real estate deals.

'Alphabet-soup' terms like CAD, CAM and CIM are common currency in the engineering data consultancy business. The last of these abbreviations has tended to remain a technical concept, slow to develop into a commercial product. It takes a long time for the initiated to discern the area of need that this concept (computer integrated manufacturing) is intended to satisfy. Briefly, they are

● less raw material tied up in production;
● less capital tied up in production; and
● lower labour costs.

Experience has taught me a healthy respect for the difficulties of understanding the trade logic of an industry I am not familiar with.

Analyses of portfolio and business unit, environment and industry

Companies, almost without exception, comprise more than one business unit. A company can therefore be said to constitute a portfolio. A portfolio may also be called a division, a sector, or something else. The important thing in working with strategy is to sort out the business make-up of the portfolio to ascertain the appropriate material for analysis.

The terms 'industry' and 'market' relate to the business unit. It is a business unit that belongs to a given industry and operates in a given market. Sometimes it may make good business sense to define more than one business unit within the same industry. A strategic sector may consist of a number of business units – in, say, the computer industry – that exhibit powerful synergy, for example in the manufacturing function.

A portfolio often includes business units operating in different industries. Apart from general environment factors, the analytical variables will then consist of the attractiveness of the industries concerned and the degree of synergy between the business units in the portfolio.

The following list will help to clarify the analytical variables for purposes of strategic analysis.

Sequence of strategy analysis
- Portfolio – company, division of sector
  - (a) non-industry-specific environmental factors
  - (b) attractiveness of industries concerned (rough assessment)
  - (c) horizontal links in the portfolio
- Business unit – company, division or sector
  - (a) industry-specific environmental factors
  - (b) market

    (c)   business units in the industry

    (d)   segmentation.

In this section we shall deal with business environment and industry, primarily with respect to the business unit. This will be followed under the heading 'analysis of the company', by one section on portfolio analysis and another on business unit analysis.

Every strategy development process dealing with a business unit must begin with an effort to understand its trade logic and to make an analysis of the market and the industry, the market being the arena in which the business unit operates.

I have found that some people think the term 'industry analysis' sounds too generalised and far-reaching. It may seem so if you do not go on from industry analysis to the specific market and follow the process through to a successfully implemented strategy. If you consider industry analysis simply as a demarcation of the ball park in which the rest of the game will be played, I think you can avoid the trap of confusing means with ends.

Figure 13 contains an illustration of how to describe an industry in meaningful terms. You do not always have to perform all the analyses. If you search the literature on strategy for all the analyses that can and should be made, you run the risk of winding up in a situation where the analysis is an end in itself, and this is something to be avoided. The correct sequence is first to look at the industry and the trade logic that governs it, and then try to form a more detailed picture of your own business unit or your own company in the context of the industry and of the market in which it operates.

An industry consists basically of a number of supplying companies selling a certain kind of product that is in demand from a certain group of customers who base their demands on certain needs. The fundamental issue of need is often overlooked, maybe because it is not included in traditional strategy models.

A good example is the way the automotive industry, as recently as the early 1970s, misinterpreted its customers' needs. It was assumed that people were rational, just as rational as the planning technocrats, and would therefore choose cars on price and performance. It was taken for granted that the customer regarded a car simply as a means of transportation, with cost-effectiveness as the sole

NEEDS	CUSTOMERS	DEMAND	PRODUCT	COMPANY	SUPPLIERS AND OTHERS INVOLVED
Structural change	What does a typical customer look like?	Is demand moving upward or downward?	Relative quality	What structural changes are taking place?	Risk of forward integration
Primary hierarchy of needs	Who are the customers and where are they?	Are there any substitute products?	Possibilities for differentiation	Strategic groups	Importance of deliveries to suppliers
How are needs differentiated?	Risk of backward integration	Can the demand be segmented?	What gives the customer added value?	Barriers to entry and exit	Social factors
			Is the product perfectly matched to the demand?	Productivity	Political factors
			Importance of product to customers	Capital structure and finance	
				Importance of marketing	
				Industry capacity versus demand	
				Profitability	
				Management capability	

Fig. 13   Market and industry structures – a proposed list of factors for analysis

criterion for choice. This led to the 'world car' trend, with mass production as the key factor – a classic example of the 'rationality trap'.

Reality has since proved that this was a total misreading of the need as car buyers perceived it, and that there are other needs not amenable to deductive logic that control the choice of a car. It often pays to look deeper into the hierarchy of needs – which can be highly complex – and determine which needs are really being satisfied.

Fig. 14 Environment versus industry. The terms market, industry and environment refer to partly overlapping phenomena that may require explanation. This figure attempts to clarify the concept of environment on a concrete level so that the subject can be discussed in a structured manner

Environmental factors external to the industry	Environmental factors specific to the industry
* Economic factors	* Importance of product to users
* Social factors	* Growth of industry (actually growth of market)
* Demographic factors	* Stability of industry, i.e. barriers to entry, exit and other changes
	* Industry-related economic factors such as raw material prices, labour costs, etc.

The boundaries of a market are defined by its customers and the industries competing for the demand generated by those customers. Its trade logic may be different in different parts of the world, unless the industry is an international one.

Let us take the Swedish building and civil engineering industry as an example. For major construction projects above a certain size, the market for Swedish companies is limited to certain parts of the world, the United States, for example, can be excluded. This can be contrasted with the building of weekend cabins, which may not even have a national market. The question, then, is what market does the company concerned actually supply.

These examples are chosen to illustrate the relativity of the market concept: you have to describe the arena you intend to fight in. That arena need not necessarily be limited to the market actually supplied, but can quite well be extended to take in territories or segments of demand which, though your own company may not be supplying them, are of great importance to some of your chief competitors and should therefore be included in the assessments on which you base your choice of strategy.

The number and purchasing power of *customers* are of great importance, especially to the marketing function. In some cases, especially where you are selling to private individuals it may be a good thing to classify typical customers by demographic or other characteristics. In industrial markets, the risk of backward integration by customers is naturallly an item of great concern. Especially in industries where the degree of change is relatively low, there is a risk of integration by both customers and suppliers. The packaging industry is a good example: a large manufacturer of, say, detergents may decide to install an in-plant packaging line, while the boxboard supplier is quite likely to integrate his operations forward by acquiring extrusion and conversion equipment to make plastic-coated board and cut it into carton blanks.

Methods of describing customers must vary according to industry. The needs of customers, or customers' customers, create a demand that must be ascertained.

One question is whether the demand is going to increase or diminish in the long term over a whole business cycle. Another important basis for classification is segmentation of demand, i.e. how the needs of various groups differ from each other.

The nature of and changes in *demand* represent one of the central areas of analysis. A study of the history of demand, with reference both to volume and to what demands exist and have existed, can be highly informative. The demands of bank customers are moving towards stock investment counseling, and the spread of this demand among different age and income groups is a good example of how the dynamics of the market change the conditions in which the industry must operate.

Many revolutionary changes are recorded in commercial history. They have often been sparked off by the appearance on the market of a substitute, defined as a means of satisfying a need by a different technology than the one used hitherto. One example is the transistor, which replaced valves in radio and television sets. An initial result was that many manufacturers stopped making radio valves, which resulted in shortages and rising prices. Keeping a constant lookout for possible substitutes for your own product is a business virtue.

On the right-hand side of Fig. 13 there are a number of *suppliers*, whose inclination to integrate forward could bear watching. Is it conceivable that a manufacturer of small two-stroke engines might start putting his own lawnmowers, outboard motors and chainsaws on the market? Are the suppliers strong enough, and is the market important enough to them, to make forward integration one of their strategic options?

The size and nature of the value-added component are often key issues in connection with forward vertical integration.

The companies in the industry are of course one of the chief ingredients in any analysis of the industry. The amount of detail in which competitors are analyzed will naturally depend on the need in each individual case. Let us briefly review some of the main groups.

One main variable is the corporate structure of the industry and the nature of its production. What strategic groups exist in the industry? Strategic groups, as stated earlier (see p. 45), are groups of companies that compete by similar methods. The number of companies in the market can be of decisive importance, as can structural development among them.

If your market is in a maturing phase of development, usually characterized by a concentration of companies, you should consider your own company's attitude to structural change with great care. Another question relating to the general structure of companies in the industry is the degree of importance attached to economies of scale. In some industries, like consumer capital goods, for instance, this is a fundamental issue.

Entry and exit barriers (see Fig. 15) are a factor of vast importance in the structural development of an industry. In the consultancy business, for example, companies never grow very big because there are very few obstacles in the way of starting new firms. The structure of the prefabricated timber-frame house industry in Sweden has likewise changed very little over a long period of time, but for a very different reason: a virtually insurmountable exit barrier. The barrier in this case consists of the keen desire of local government authorities to maintain employment in their communities, as a result of which bankrupt companies, until quite recently, were sold for a nominal sum and carried on operating with virtually no capital costs.

Productivity, capital structure and finance are analytical elements that have sometimes been neglected by the newer school of strategic thought. Yet the way capital is employed is always of great interest, and productivity is of decisive importance in some industries.

Fig. 15 Barriers

---

1   ENTRY BARRIERS

* *Economics of scale* – high investment needed to achieve low production costs
* *Differentiated product* – customers loyal to one brand or supplier
* *Capital requirement* – a lot of capital needed for credits, image, etc.
* *Changeover costs* – cost to customer of changing suppliers
* *Distribution channels* – none available
* *Components or raw materials* – deliveries unobtainable
* *Location already occupied*
* *Lack of experience* and know-how
* *Expected opposition* – competitors likely to react strongly
* *Price-cutting*
* *Patents*

2   EXIT BARRIERS

* *Write-off of heavy investments*
* *Prestige and image*
* *Management ego*
* *High disengagement costs* – e.g. for restoring site to original condition
* *Trade union opposition*
* *Shared costs* – that will have to be borne by some other product or market
* *Suppliers, customers, distributors*

The average profitability of the industry can be taken as a benchmark against which a company's performance should be measured. One of the goals of strategy is to achieve a sustained level of profitability that is above the industry average.

To understand the trade logic of an industry it is necessary to identify the key factors for success. An analysis of the value-added component – how it arises and what it consists of – is often a useful exercise here. To be able to grasp the key factors you must understand the structure of needs in the industry and market concerned. If you clearly recognize the need structures that underly demand, you have come a long way towards establishing effective business strategies. I have seen examples of corporate managements who have

68

entered complicated industries as newcomers and have gotten into serious trouble just because they failed to identify the key factors for success.

The *total capacity of industry* in a given market as compared to existing demand is often a self-evident and well-known quantity, but not always. Changes in industrial capacity over a period of time and plans for the future can be useful pointers in strategy work. The expansion plans of shipyards and carmakers provide two examples of whole industries that have overestablished themselves. People with foresight realized at an early stage what was going to happen, and avoided bad investments.

Management competence, both in competing companies and in your own, is hard to measure in exact terms, but is one of the most important variables in the strategic arena. The ability of your executives and the strategic orientation of your principal competitors are items that must be considered in an analysis of the industry.

Studies of *product* should concentrate on analysing what your own company is offering, but must also be placed in the frame of reference of industry standards. The matter of product is dealt with rather summarily in traditional strategic analysis, but the PIMS model (see p. 172) includes an assessment of relative product quality, i.e. a comparison between one's own product and its three biggest competitors. The model includes both product-related and service-related variables.

In a market analysis the differentiation of the industry's products can be compared with the segmentation of needs of the customer side. Economic value to the customer is a point of great importance in some industries. For a packaging company, the economic value to the customer may sometimes be small, consisting solely in the customer's interest in getting his product put into consumer packs at lowest possible cost. Other companies may use packaging as a means of differentiating their products, and will therefore be less price-sensitive.

One of the standard techniques of modern strategy development is to match the product to customer demand. This apparently obvious relationship is however easily lost sight of when companies grow bigger and more bureaucratic, and the focus of their attention is diverted from their customers to other things like their own production apparatus or their personnel.

In this section on industries and markets I want to emphasize the need for variation in the way the analysis is made. A template or checklist for every conceivable analytical factor is every industry would be cumbersome to construct. So what is needed is a creative approach to the key questions of strategy in the specific industry concerned. Let me conclude this section with a couple of examples:

Data consultancy is a growth industry almost everywhere. Unlike almost every other industry, the key issue of strategy in data consultancy is how to get hold of the necessary production resources, i.e. people. Once a consultancy firm has managed to get good people on its payroll, the problem shifts to that of keeping them. This is, to put it mildly, difficult, because skilled consultants are the industry's strategic resource and can therefore parlay up their salaries by letting a competitor hire them away.

However, in many countries supply is now catching up with demand, so the rules for succeeding in this industry are changing. This change in the industry-specific environment is likely to lead to structural changes within the next ten years.

The airfreight industry had been trying for a long time to differentiate its product, but in many cases had failed to understand the underlying need factors in the business. 'Package deals' or 'courier services' were constructed in an effort to secure partly new kinds of business by offering a product resembling what airlines were most familiar with, namely carrying passengers. Many airlines, however, lacked an appreciation of the true character of airfreight as a business-to-business service and of the underlying needs, and therefore often offered the wrong product.

Analysis of the company

We shall now leave industries and markets and go on to consider the company itself. The analysis of one's own company falls into two main parts. First we must make a general analysis of the business units of which the company is composed, and then we must be able to position each of the business units relative to its respective industry. As an industry analysis, the analysis of both a portfolio and a business unit can be made as comprehensive as you want it to be. The problem lies rather in limiting its scope to the items of greatest relevance in the individual case.

Portfolio analysis

The first object of a portfolio analysis is to be able to 'compare apples with bananas', i.e. to find a frame of reference that can be used as a basis for assessing the component business units of the portfolio in order to obtain the necessary data for decisions on structural changes, changes in executive management teams, etc.

The second object is to chart existing horizontal links to see whether they can be better utilized to gain competitive advantages for the portfolio as a whole.

Portfolio strategy is not just a matter of acquiring or getting rid of business units, though this is an important part of such strategies. Just as the elements of strategy serve as means of expression for business units, there are corresponding strategic elements in a portfolio strategy. Above all there are four items which are essential in the formulation of a portfolio strategy:

Corporate mission

There must be a concensus of agreement on what the business unit's corporate mission is to be, and on what goals and what strategic direction the business should be given. Thus the corporate management must insist that the business units – usually subsidiary companies – are managed in a strategic manner.

Results and expectations

Results must of course be demanded in the form of increased sales, market shares, productivity, profitability, revenue generation, R&D, and maybe other goals. Some of these will be numerical with clearly defined contours, while others will be 'softer' and less readily quantifiable.

Demarcation lines and links

To control synergies and interactions with other units in the portfolio, you need a set of standards and rules for management systems, dealing between subsidiaries, etc. Competitive situations, if any, should be clarified and crystal-clear directives issued concerning lines of demarcation. Links that benefit the whole must be identified, described and exploited.

Allocation of resources

This can be a question of investing in profitable business ideas, supplying skilled management capacity, setting up a joint international sales organization for the whole group, or other resources that may be supplied or needed by the component business units.

Many diversified corporations give no strategic impulses to their business units. This applies particularly to corporations of the conglomerate type in which several established companies which bear little relation to each other have been lumped together as subsidiaries of a passive holding company.

The presssure to generate short-term profits and positive cash flows is often so great that the parent company cannot provide its various business units with investment capital. It is also difficult, time-consuming and usually expensive to build up joint resources. The risk of short-sightedness in financial conglomerates is acute, which of course should be a memento to the professional manager.

The factors that make it possible to compare different business units with each other, regardless of industry, are of course key criteria of various kinds. They can be said to fall into two groups:

● operational skill
● strategic attractiveness.

Figure 16 is a graphic representation of such an analysis. I have chosen to show the PIMS analysis (profit impact of market strategy), which is admirably suited to this purpose. (See also the discussion of PIMS in the Appendix).

'Operational skill' here means the *actual profit level* compared to what PIMS calls 'PAR ROI', i.e. a profit level that is normal with reference to the strategic situation (ROI – 'return on investment'). The first criterion of operational skill is the expected return on investment with reference to the strategic situation of the business unit. The second criterion is how divergence from ROI varies over a period of time. The third is productivity, assessed as added value per employee, compared to average productivity, and the fourth is the productivity trend compared with average productivity.

'Strategic attractiveness' is a measure of growth potential assessed on *relative market share* and *relative product quality*. Other criteria are the growth trend of the industry and attractiveness to investors, judged according to certain subcriteria derived from a number of the world's stock exchanges.

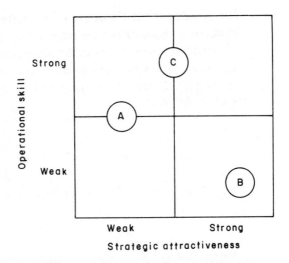

Fig. 16 PIMS portfolio analysis. Business unit A has mediocre operational skill (capability) and a weak strategic position. It is obviously desirable to try to move this unit in a 'north-easterly' direction. Business unit C is strong operationally, but its strategic attractiveness is only middling. This unit is probably earning quite a lot of money, and unless the portfolio management thinks its strategic position can be improved, they should consider selling it off while it is still in good shape. Business unit B is a candidate for a radical 'management transplant'. Its strategic position is strong but its operative management is poor; this situation in fact represents an opportunity that ought to be seized

Even if you do not have access to such a rich database as the one PIMS uses, you can apply the same technique in somewhat modified form by plotting the company's position on one axis and the attractiveness of the industry on the other. The company's position can be assessed on criteria such as:

- market share
- growth rate
- profitability
- technological status
- image
- management skill

For the other axis, attractiveness of the industry, you can use other criteria like:

- industry growth
- profitability trend
- competitive structure
- position of the industry on the maturity curve.

It is evident that this type of analysis basically calls for subjective judgements of where business units should be placed in the coordinate scheme. Operations research naturally find it hard to accept this kind of evaluation, and we therefore find attempts being made in various strategic models to quantify the criteria. As long as you are aware of the weaknesses of the methodology, this is an excellent aid to positioning the business units in a portfolio. You should use it only as a technique for arranging a bouquet of business units relative to each other, while resisting the temptation to use it as a platform for developing strategies for individual business units.

Analysis of a business unit using the elements of strategy

It is of course difficult to decide exactly what part of a company analysis is of an operational nature and what has strategic implications. As in the case of industry analysis, the number of variables is practically unlimited. This is particularly true if you include all the 'soft' variables which have a proven bearing on the commercial success of the business.

One example of how the importance of a given variable can vary is the production or EDP function. In most cases it is absolutely essential that production maintains a reasonable level of productivity compared with the industry as a whole. However, that does not necessarily mean that productivity is important in terms of business strategy, unless the company's performance is below average for its industry or an opportunity exists for a productivity breakthrough that could offer a sustainable strategic advantage.

Part of the same reasoning is applicable to the EDP function. This is usually an auxiliary function which is expected to work smoothly, and is thus not important from a business strategy point of view in normal circumstances. The situation is radically different, however, in cases where the EDP function can supply the competitive edge needed to improve profitability. The data strategy view, about which I shall have more to say later, is being more and more widely used as a means of gaining a competitive edge, e.g. by giving better customer access or by creating entry barriers.

At one time, strategic thinking was totally dominated by the analytical component. Now the pendulum has swung the other way, so that presently there is an exaggerated tenden-

74

cy to deprecate analysis. The question is simply what analyses should be made out of the wide choice available.

PIMS is my own favourite among all the methods deriving from operations research. The danger of using PIMS, as with all similar tools, is that analytical results can all too easily influence the conclusions and inhibit creativity in determining strategies – something the true strategist must resist with all his might.

The ideal, then, is to perform an analysis that satisfactorily elucidates the present position and development trends as a basis for intelligent predictions.

If the market and industry analyses are performed by talented people with strategic experience and creative gifts, they will yeild an understanding of the business that will enable an analysis of the company to be made in a much more cost-effective way than would otherwise be possible. Thus at the corporate analysis stage you will not need to analyse everything in sight; instead you can concentrate on the industry's key variables and the deviations, positive or negative, exhibited by the company or business unit under study.

In making the company analysis, you would of course base the selection of variables on the elements or expressions of strategy. Recall from the previous chapter that these elements are:

1. corporate mission
2. competitive edge
3. business organization
4. product
5. development programmes
6. acquisitions and disinvestments
7. resources: investments and costs
8. management competence and culture
9. markets

One of the decisive steps in company analysis is an analysis of profitability, capital structure and financing. There are of course problems if the business unit in question is not a separate legal entity and does not have its own profit-and-loss account and balance sheet. However, I believe that analysis of profit-and-loss accounts and balance sheets is so important that if they are not available to begin with, you could sit down and draw them up for the preceding two of three years.

In addition to the nine elements of strategy, then, there are at least three other items to consider:

- analysis of profitability
- analysis of productivity
- analysis of information system efficiency.

Here follows a brief commentary on the application of each of these twelve analytical variables in corporate analysis:

Profitability

Profitability in some industries is chronically low because of overestablishment. Packaging companies in Europe, for example, have a hard time making a satisfactory ROI. This is due partly to continent-wide overcapacity, and partly to the insignificant value that packaging adds to a product. A company's profitability must thus be judged in the context of its industry.

The importance of the rate of capital turnover is generally underrated in Europe, whose industries often have more capital tied up in their operations than their counterparts in the USA and Japan. An analysis of balance sheets can give useful information; you should particularly look for assets unrelated to the business, and for opportunities to increase the rate of capital turnover in the form of goods, and generally try to speed up the movement of capital (invoicing over balance-sheet total).

Figure 17 was drawn by my colleague Hans Thornell. It admirably illustrates the relationship between type of capital and ROI requirement. Assets are supposed to generate a surplus that will both cover the cost of financing and produce a growth in equity. Generating goodwill means a poorer return on investment. The credit items in the example consist partly of interest-free supplier credits and partly of latent tax debts on untaxed reserves. Creative work with the basic elements of the balance often yields valuable clues to strategy.

Productivity

The new emphasis on business development and more rigorous revenue parameters have placed entirely new demands on production. Long runs and low unit costs are no

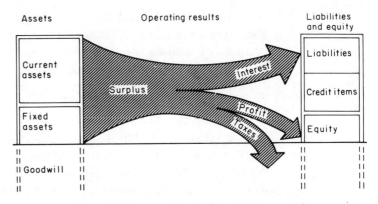

Fig. 17 The profit concept with reference to the balance sheet

longer obvious goals. On the contrary, a market-oriented strategy often calls for the very opposite. The packaging industry's customers, i.e. food manufacturing companies, want to be able to differentiate their products and therefore change the appearance of their packs more often. This generates a demand for shorter production runs.

The growing importance of capital costs relative to freight costs also provides a push in the direction of smaller lots and shorter runs, creating a demand for flexibility in retooling.

The purchase of Airbus aircraft by SAS is another example of how easy it is to fall into the economies-of-scale trap. The idea here was to put one large aircraft on, say, the Stockholm–Copenhagen route with one departure instead of maybe three DC-9 flights at hourly intervals. Market orientation, however, means giving passengers a choice of departure times: that is why the Airbuses were replaced by smaller aircraft.

The same kind of rethinking is now being applied to the gigantic car service stations by the big car companies. People do not feel at home in these factory-like complexes, and we shall certainly see a return to smaller units.

The productivity of a company as compared to others in the same industry and a creative analysis of opportunities for gaining strategic advantages in production are two important elements of analysis. Productivity should be expressed as value added in relation to labour and capital. An understanding of the make-up and origins of the value-added component can provide valuable insights.

Information system efficiency

There is a strong tendency for people in some auxiliary

functions to develop a culture resulting in greater loyalty to their own area of specialization and to colleagues in other companies than to the company that employs them. One place where this tends to happen is in the EDP (information systems) function, perhaps because the demand for qualified EDP personnel exceeds the supply.

The EDP function is often less oriented towards its own internal customers than is the case in other functions. The EDP function is moreover of fundamental importance to a company's ability to measure the success of its strategies. The EDP side, like production, is of great importance on the purely operational plane.

In addition, the EDP function is more and more often acquiring strategic importance in that it can provide a competitive edge in a growing number of cases. Thus EDP, again like production, can prove to be a fruitful field for the creative explorer in search of strategic advantages.

Corporate mission

A review of the make-up of the corporate mission is a specially important part of strategic analysis. Not only does the corporate mission comprise needs, product, customers and competitors but, as the name implies, it also gives a picture of how people in the company view their mission in the world of business.

Quite often one finds corporate missions expressed something like this:

'The ABC company will manufacture, market and sell products, X, Y and Z and with good profitability.'

This type of formulation is common, though maybe not in quite such an exaggerated form. It reveals a lack of customer orientation and an unhealthily introverted view of the company's business.

The product is listed as a separate variable among the elements of strategy, while customers are included in the market element and competitors come under the analysis of environment, industry and market. In this context, therefore, attention should be focused on the analysis of needs and on the attitudes to customers and business that the corporate mission expresses.

A survey of customer's needs is an absolutely essential task for the strategic leader. In my opinion there is no other single variable that can compare in importance with an understanding of the structure of customers' needs. It is often the very key to determination of strategy.

Management awareness of the corporate mission gives a clear indication of how clearly strategy is defined and, by the same token, of how competent the managament is in the area of strategy.

Competitive edge

The object of strategic analysis is to obtain the best possible input for a choice of strategy that will secure a strategic advantage or competitive edge leading to a long-term improvement in profitability. The aim is to make the company more profitable than the rest of its industry, and keep it that way for as long as possible. A competitive edge can be found in any one of a great number of functions, or can be just as likely be the result of a combination of several functions.

The most creative part of company analysis is in fact the search for a competitive edge. The real question in this context is: 'If I were a potential customer, why should I buy from you rather than from somebody else?'

Organization

The essential question in connection with organization and its struture in strategy analysis is how well the organization matches the structure of the business. Is the organization optimally subdivided (differentiated) with reference to the structure of the business, i.e. to portfolio, business units and functions?

Divisionalization can result in organizational structures that do not always reflect business structures. One division of a large plant-engineering corporation was engaged in contracting operations on a global scale, and one department of that division sold components used in the plants. These components were distributed through wholesalers, which meant that the department was operating according to a business logic totally alien to that of the division as a whole.

Differentiation on the basis of business units is important, but so is integration on the basis of links within a portfolio. I once saw an example where a bank differentiated itself on the basis of its customers' needs and by doing so achieved a tremendous business drive that very quickly boosted its profits. This differentiation will be beneficial even in steady-state conditions, provided that operations can be integrated in such a way as to take advantage of existing links and optimize the whole.

Product

A company's product generally consists of a range of goods and services (hardware and software). The software component is tending to become more and more important nowadays, even in hardware-type industries. The product can be analysed on the basis of customers' needs with reference to changes in composition, rate of change, and substitutes. In some industries, product renewal is a key strategic factor. In 'private banking', i.e. the services that banks offer to private persons, the rate of renewal has often been remarkably low; new products on this market have been launched by other companies. In fact product renewal often comes from newly started companies or from companies outside the established industry.

One of the most essential elements of strategy is the way in which a product can be renewed to keep it more closely attuned to changes in the structure of customers' needs.

Development programmes

A company's development programmes say a lot about its strategic course. Though development could be dealt with under the heading of resources (see below), I feel that this is a matter of sufficient importance to be treated as a separate element of strategy.

The term 'development' is of course used here in its widest sense. It can refer to products, markets or people. Development programmes are often booked as overheads, and it therefore takes a very close reading of profit-and-loss accounts to identify them once they have been defined in individual cases. The size of the total commitment to development, and how the size of that commitment varies over a period of time, are very interesting items of information.

Structural changes: acquisition and disinvestment

One suggestion for an approach is that you go back three years and examine changes in the make-up of the portfolio during that time. The character of the changes naturally give valuable information on which way the portfolio is moving. Structural changes generally occur in parts of the portfolio. It is rarer for functional parts of business units to be bought or sold.

This has recently started to happen to EDP functions, however. Some major Swedish corporations, for example, have set up joint venture companies in partnership with computer software houses and farmed out their information-processing functions to the new companies. One suspects that the companies who have done this have simply capitulated in the face of difficulties in keeping EDP costs under control and matching the output of the EDP function to their needs.

There is a danger, however, in abandoning an important function that could be the source of a future strategic advantage.

Resources: investments and costs

The definition of strategy states that it is an integrated pattern of actions designed to guide a company's resources in a given direction. If you define one of the elements of strategy as 'resources', as I do, that can include almost anything.

The idea, however, is by reviewing *investment decisions* over a period of years and by studying essential items in the *development of total costs* to form a clear picture of preferences in the strategic course followed up to now.

Whether a decision to spend money shows up as a cost item on the profit-and-loss account or as an investment on the balance sheet is of minor importance in this context: the important thing is to look at how money has been spent on market development, buildings, machinery, the sales force, personnel, R&D, etc.

A survey of the trends in total resource utilization gives valuable information about management ambitions and goals.

Management competence and culture

The clarity with which a management is able to communicate its corporate mission, vision, level of ambition and current strategies gives an indication of that management's strategic competence. This does not of course mean that the information has to be presented textbook-fashion, but rather that the management must have a feeling for these important isues and be able to make its feeling understood.

Subjective judgements such as attitudes to risk, business-manship and entrepreneurship, preferences in the hiring of executives, attitudes to customers and employees, attitudes to the quality of the product and other 'soft' factors, when taken together, can provide vital clues to the prospects for future accomplishment.

Many companies still rate team compatibility higher than drive and performance motivation. People with the former characteristic are 'nice guys', which those with the latter often are not. But the latter are often outstandingly success-ful in business, which the former are not. Evaluation of businessmanship, intelligence, energy, education, etc. gives the strategist essential information.

Markets

Market analysis is well developed in industries that deal in fast-moving consumer goods. The farther away you get from that category of product, the less market analysis you tend to find. In the previous chapter I mentioned a technique called marketing audit that can be used for a critical evaluation of the efficiency of the marketing function. In strategy analysis it is rather a matter of surveying the market and the custom-ers that the company is trying to sell its products to. The criteria chosen for segmentation of the market are of special interest, as adaptation of the product to the needs of diffe-rent segments is a key issue in strategy.

Segementation is in fact one of the high arts of strategy. If you can correctly distinguish those parts of a total market that have special needs, you have the key to the creation of a strategic advantage, which is the whole object of strategy.

There are actually two quite distinct parts to market analysis. The first part is quantitative: it deals with growth, maturity, geographical coverage and similar matters. The second part is more qualitative, being concerned with aspects like customer-perceived quality, customer needs and shifts in demand.

Conclusion

If you are involved in a strategy development process, it is wisest to make a thorough analysis of the basic elements and, on the basis of the results, discuss what supplementary analyses are needed. A PDS (problem detection study) or other customer-need-oriented study is fairly expensive to set up, but it can give you an unequalled guide to changes in what is possibly the most important of all the elements of strategy, namely the make-up of the product.

Depending on how complicated the product is and how many customers there are, you can choose between a statistical analysis and in-depth personal interviews. The latter are the obvious choice if you want to investigate the structure of need for, say, nuclear power plants or steel girder bridges, whereas needs having to do with the use of perfume or the merits of different grades of flour for baking are probably more amenable to statistical treatment.

It is understandable if the cost of a study of needs gives pause, but it can pay handsome dividends.

> A European airline's cargo operation accounted for 17% of its total turnover. This operation made use of space in the bodies of aircraft in symbiosis with the company's principal business, which was carrying passengers, and the contribution of freight to the coverage of fixed costs exceeded the total consolidation profit. Cargo began to lose market shares, and its profitability was considered too low after distribution of fixed costs. An anlaysis of needs revealed that uncertaintly of delivery time was the main problem for intercontinental customers; it could take anything between two and twenty days for a shipment to arrive in Singapore. The picture in Europe was entirely different: there the airline was embroiled in fierce competion from surface carriers (trucking firms), and time from door to door was the key strategic factor.
>
> The product was adjusted according to the analysis of needs. Intercontinental customers were offered a money-back guarantee of delivery on schedule, while for Europe the company constructed a door-to-door product with guaranteed delivery in less than 18 hours. These changes in the product were successful.

The foregoing example illustrates the values of a correct analysis of customer needs.

4 The strategic process – determination of strategy and implementation

Determination of strategy

Strategic advantage

The whole purpose of strategy development is to secure a strategic advantage (or competitive edge). That strategic advantage should be applicable as soon as possible, it should be as great as possible, and it should last as long as possible. A strategic advantage ought to generate 'abnormal profits', i.e. profits above the average for the industry concerned.

In Fig. 18 period A represents the time taken to formulate a strategic advantage, and period B the time during which competitors continue to operate according to their old strategies. The length of period B is a function of the type of industry concerned and its dynamic characteristics. There is of course a great difference in reaction times between, say, service-producing companies and heavy engineering industries.

Period C represents the time it takes the competition to overcome the strategic advantage. D on the vertical axis, finally, represents the magnitude of the strategic advantage. This can be expressed for example as percentage points above the industry average for return on investment.

The competitive structure of the industry sets definite limits to what can be accomplished. Some industries have an intrinsically low level of profitability. The reason may be that both the barriers to entry and the economic value to the customer are low, so that it is constantly exposed to invasion, i.e. integration by both suppliers and customers. The packaging industry is a typical example.

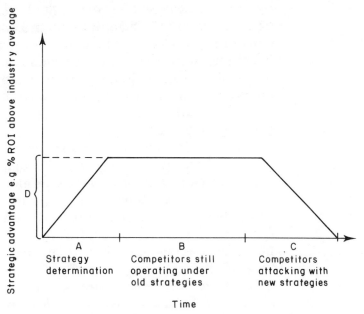

Fig. 18 Strategic advantage

Every manager should try to recognize clearly just how much room for manoeuvre he really has. Environmental constraints are more severe in some industries than in others. Generally speaking there are four kinds of environmental factors to take into account:

1. nature of needs and importance of product to customers;
2. growth trend of the industry;
3. stability of the industry (entry and exit barriers);
4. inflation factors (raw material prices, etc.).

These factors are not normally under the company's control and therefore restrict its freedom of action. You need to understand these limitations in order to utilize the possibilities that do exist of devising realistic strategies that can be put into practice with high efficiency. If you happen to be in an industry whose product is of low economic value to its customers, there is naturally nothing to stop you devoting your efforts to innovation in order to differentiate your product and thereby enhance its value-added component.

Requirements for strategy determination

A fact that has not been universally recognized is that the determination (formulation) of strategy calls for a large measure of creativity, i.e. the ability to think boldly and originally and so to find unconventional answers that lead more quickly to success in business. Anybody who makes this claim, as I have had occasion to do several times, almost invariably hears the objection that this is all very well for business development situations, but hardly applicable to defensive strategies, strategies for industries in decline or 'end game' strategies.

The objection is not relevant. There are splendid examples of how creativity has improved the competitive position of companies in depressed industries. Unfortunately, industries with problems tend to reject creative people, which accelerates the growth of the problems. However, creativity has its given place in strategy determination regardless of the strategic situation in which the company or industry finds itself.

Of all the steps in the strategy development process, strategy determination is the hardest to describe. The reason is of course that it contains a large element of indefinite creativity and situation-related process techniques controlled by the concrete facts of the situation.

Strategy should be determined by a fairly small group of individuals including representatives of those who have performed the analyses, members of the top management, and preferably someone such as a consultant acting in a catalytic role. The analysts should take part and should be available for consultation throughout the strategy determintion process, but they should not have a decisive say in discussions of the choice of strategy. The question of who should be present at a strategy determinaion is thus controlled to no small degree by individual personality factors.

It is not possible in real life to draw up rules for how a strategy should be determined. The answer takes shape in the mind(s) of one or a few individuals upon whom rests the ultimate responsibility for the long-term development of the business. I have been present on occasions where the decision was made at a seminar a few weeks after the analyses had been presented; but I have also heard strategies decided informally on a balcony in the sun.

In fact the choice of principal strategy is often made informally, but that is not to say that it should not be speedily referred to the whole of the company's top management for modification and sharpening. The responsible leader should take the opportunity to sound out those people around him whose judgement he trusts, to test his own views on the strategic options available or the alternative that he himself advocates.

The quality of strategy determination is controlled by three factors:

- the quality of the analysis;
- the strategic experience of the people involved; and
- business creativity.

Analysis was formerly by far the most powerful factor in strategy determination. Strategic management ability is, as I have said before, a matter of concrete strategic experience and ability to abstract from it. Most corporate executives encounter very few strategic situations during their lifetimes, and part of the purpose of training in strategic leadership is to give executives experience in the form of awareness of different strategic situations.

Creativity cannot be produced to order. The choice of environment and the right tone set by the leader of the debate are factors that have a large influence in encouraging creative thinking.

Modern research on creativity has shown that providing opportunities for hard enough and long enough concentration is a decisive factor for success in generating ideas. We are talking here about time measured by the calender, which means that periods of intense concentration must be interleaved with periods for allowing ideas to ripen to the point where they will repay renewed concentration.

Uncontrolled creativity is of little value in strategic work. Creativity must be disciplined and channelled to avoid long discussion of trivialities. There is a tendency on the part of many people to equate creativity with some sort of wild brainstorming unconnected with the hard facts of life. The dividing line between a successful entrepreneur and an undisciplined enthusiast is sometimes very fine indeed. The kind of creativity we are talking about here is the ability to integrate known items of knowledge into new patterns.

Lines of thought in strategy determination

There are a number of strategic check questions that can stimulate debate in the strategy determination phase. I have listed some of them here in the hope that they can provide useful impulses for discussion of concrete cases.

1. *What tricks might fate play on us?* Are there other ways

of satisfying the customer needs we are looking at that could be realised by a conceivable technological advance? Are there other changes afoot in classic environmental factors that may be relevant to our choice of strategy?

Environmental factors external to the industry are

- economic
- social
- demographic
- political.

Environmental factors specific to the industry, factors over which the individual company has little or no control, are:

- importance of the product to customers;
- rate of growth of the industry
- stability of the industry (entry and exit barriers and other changes); and
- industry-related economic factors like raw material prices, wage inflation, etc.

2. *Is the corporate mission outdated?* A corporate mission always relates to a certain need experienced by certain customers at a certain time. Neither the market nor its needs are static: they are dynamic. The structure of needs therefore changes gradually, so that in time a corporate mission may become obsolete. Large organizations sometimes fail to notice ongoing changes, and consequently fail to adapt their corporate mission to changing times.

3. *Product differentiation?* There may be opportunities for differentiation that run counter to the production function's desire for low unit costs. The possibilities of further differentiation of the product should be given a critical examination (see the next section on product differentiation).

4. *Software component of the product?* There is a tendency, especially in hardware-oriented industries, to underrate the importance of peripheral services. Empirical research emphatically confirms the assertion that hardware-type industries *always* underestimate the importance of the software component to their customers. Conversely, this means that the customer's choice of supplier is guided by the software or service component of the product to a much higher degree than suppliers realize. An increase in the quantity or an improvement

88

in the quality of the software component can in fact be regarded as a special case of product differentiation.

5. *How can profitability be boosted above the industry average?* A pointer that is often useful is to try and find out what makes a company more profitable than the others in its industry. It could be a matter of identifying differentiated needs, of investing in special production facilities, or of finding a geographical market where the pressure of competition is less. Profitability in many industries is unsatisfactory from the point of view of return on investment, and in those industries the question is even more relevant. Understanding the value added and what makes it valuable to the customer is an important starting point.

6. *System sales?* Can software and hardware be combined in such a way as to let us assume a greater functional responsibility for the product than is usual in the industry? This is another variation on the theme of product differentiation.

7. *Vertical division of labour?* Should we try to take over some functions from customers or suppliers, or should we give up some of our functions to them? A lowcost furniture store chain chose to leave assembly of the furniture to its customers, while taking over the design and production planning functions from its suppliers. A free-for-all is going on in the freight industry, with freight agents trying to take over shippers' functions, customers trying to integrate forward and be their own freight agents, freight agents acquiring their own fleets of vehicles and carriers setting up as freight agents. In situations where the economic value of the product to the customer is low, the boundary functions in the vertical integration chain are apt to become bones of contention.

8. *Is there an ideal company to emulate?* If so, it could be worth studying. There may be such an 'ideal company' located at a safe distance on another continent, far enough away not to be a competitor. In the airfreight industry, advanced systems are being used by American carriers who are not in competition with European airlines and can therefore be taken as examples by the latter. It can be worth while to pay for access to somebody else's know-how – and the company you study is usually flattered by your willingness to learn from it.

9. *Can strategic groups be identified?* Strategic groups can often be a useful basis for catergorization, depending on the industry. An industry can be divided into strategic groups according to quality as perceived by the customer, method of distribution, technology, or some other variable that can be regarded as a key factor in the industry concerned.

> Electric hand tools are used for example by both professionals and private persons, and differ considerably in both design and manufacture. Companies in this industry can quite easily be divided into two groups: those who sell through trade distributors to professional users, and those who sell through the retail trade to private persons.

10. *What would be the best of possible worlds?* A company can conceive of an ideal state of affairs that is not a practical option in real life. Where the level of ambition is low or ability to think in strategic terms is lacking, that best of possible worlds may never even be discussed. I was recently involved in a project to restructure a Swedish industry whose price levels were 40% below those in other countries as a result of destructive competition.

11. *What are the crucial issues?* They need to be identified and elucidated when strategy determination is discussed. Which are the few but vital problems that need to be solved because they are blocking the healthy development of the company?

12. *What are the barriers?* Barriers are important as both friends and enemies. Entry barriers can be your enemies when you are trying to break into a new segment. Exit barriers can be your enemies when competitors you are trying to get rid of fail to leave the field as expected. But barriers can be your friends in the reverse cases. If you have succeeded in occupying a favourable position, you should try to erect barriers as quickly as possible to protect your strategic advantage for as long as possible. Thinking through barriers of various kinds is an important part of strategy determination (see Fig. 15).

13. *Can information systems be used as a strategic weapon?* Modern information technology has a growing potential for use as a means of differentiating products and building barriers. There are now companies that specialize in making other companies more competitive

with the help of information systems. There are three dimensions to think in:

- Who is the information system aimed at? Customers, suppliers or competitors?
- What function does the system perform? Processing, storage or distribution of data?
- How does it affect your product? Cost, innovation, differentiation, barriers, quality, verification of need and demand?

> An example: a freight company operating a fleet of distribution trucks differentiated its product by reporting on the delivery status of all its shipments, a service that was appreciated by customers in connection with emergency shipments, delays or wrong shipments.
>
> Another example: the use of information systems by the US Government during the air traffic controller strike. According to Harley Schaiken of MIT, information systems gave the Government a decisive advantage in breaking the strike.

Differentiation

In modern strategy development there is a dominant dichotomy between cost effectiveness and differentiation. A well-known exponent of this is Michael Porter, who distinguishes between three general strategies: cost advantage, differentiation and focusing.

Another example is the consultancy firm Strategic Planning Associates (SPA), who maintain that a competitive edge consists in either lower cost for the producer or greater value for the customer. According to them, the fundamental choice for management is whether to compete on price or on value. They use a simple quadrant matrix in which one axis stands for price sensitivity and the other for product mystique, i.e. the extent to which customers discern distinctions between the products of different suppliers in the industry.

> As I see it, differentiation is really an expression of a company's effort to project itself as unique in some respect, be it in product characteristics, in range of peripheral services or in price.

If we adopt this assumption we can proceed to discuss how our own company can project itself as unique in any respect.

The starting point for any discussion of differentiation should be a thorough analysis of possible criteria for segmentation.

> A segment is a part of a total market that differs from the rest of the total market in its needs or its buying behaviour.

Segmentation is an essential clue to determining the scope of competition in an industry, or what parts of a market a company should aim to serve and how. Segmentation of an industry also reveals those parts of it that are poorly served either by competitors or by your own company.

Finding a new way to segment the market that leads to better identification of customers' needs often offers a splendid opportunity to gain a competitive edge. Some of the key questions in this context are:

1. Can we add anything further of value to our product?
2. Can we reduce the number of functions?
3. Are there any other combinations of goods and services that satisfy the need better?
4. Are there any other technologies or patterns of need satisfaction?

You can work with segmentation matrices with buyers' needs (or other customer-related yardsticks such as buyer category, distribution channel or geography) on one axis and products (divided into goods and services) on the other. Here are a few examples:

> A national Law Society found that it was poorly supported by its members. They in turn were beginning to run into hitherto unknown difficulties in the way of having to work harder and harder to maintin a constant standard of living. A survey of the members' market revealed that it fell into three distinct segments; the criterion for segmentation in this case (due to the peculiar taxation rules of the country concerned) was the method of payment for lawyers' services. The segments were:
>
> 1. legal entities (corporations), who paid lawyers' fees out of untaxed income;
> 2. the public sector, which paid out under legal aid and court-appointed counsel schemes;
> 3. private persons, who paid lawyers' fees out of taxed income (i.e. a heavily devalued currency) or through legal aid insurance policies.

Awareness of the way the market was segmented gave the Law Society valuable clues to a choice of strategy for serving its members' needs more effectively.

Laker Airways started out by specializing strictly in the segment of the market whose chief demand was for low-price transatlantic air travel. The product was characterized by simplicity, with no frills whatsoever. By segmentation, Laker was able to satisfy a specific unfulfilled need. Gradually, however, Laker began to upgrade its level of peripheral service. This made its position indistinct to buyers, which eventually led to disaster.

Correct segmentation is often the key that unlocks the door to successful product differentiation. Segments, however, are not static: a division that is relevant today may no longer be relevant a few years from now. One instance is the way dealers have begun to appear in industries where direct sales were formerly the rule. Ball-bearing wholesalers, for example, are a new but increasingly common phenomenon. Dealers nearly always have a technology of their own that demands a different selling approach – something that engineering manufacturers do not always realize.

As I mentioned before, segmentation is something of an art. So successful segmentation that leads to a differentiation of the product is not the result of an ordinary deductive process; it often demands large measures of creativity and lateral thinking.

The degree of product mystique is naturally a key factor in the context of differentiation.

> Differentiation means that a company tries to make itself unique in its industry in respect of some variable along some vector that is highly valued by its customers.

The nature of the value can be difficult to identify. In an earlier section I spoke of the competition between personal computers, mobile telephones and turbocharged cars as status symbols. High-tech companies have another kind of product mystique that is sometimes called image and represents a subjective reality as perceived by the outside world. Image has an unfortunate tendency to overbalance in one of two directions. If a company is perceived as successful, its image of success can be exaggerated to an almost grotesque degree. One example is People Express at the height of its glory. Another is SAS in Scandinavia. Conversely, a company can acquire an exceedingly bad image if it runs into trouble. This has happened to both the companies I just mentioned, as well as to a number of other high-tech companies.

It is all too easy for companies in high-tech industries to be wafted away on an inflated image of success as long as all goes well, and to start believing the myth that the outside world has built up around them. The pride that flourishes so readily in such circumstances has almost invariably gone before a fall.

In some industries like consultancy, it is just as important in deciding on marketing activities to be aware of one's own image as it is to know the true value of what one is selling to customers. This is especially true in cases where the supplier's influence on the buyer's revenue and cost structure is subjective, indirect or otherwise hard to quantify – even when the number of first-time buyers is high and the frequency of repeat orders is low. Other industries in which image is crucially important are perfumery and advocacy. The outsider's perception of reality is obviously a decisive factor when a person or company has to decide who they want to represent them in court or perform other legal services.

The term 'strategic stalemate' describes what happens when a company tries to sit on several stools at once and position itself in more than one way. A good example is People Express, which clearly occupied the position of being *the* low-price domestic air carrier in the United States. When People Express tried to occupy another position by introducing a Business Class, it just confused its customers; they found it more and more difficult to identify precisely what People Express stood for.

This brings us naturally to the concept of *positioning*, which is akin to differentiation.

The pitfalls of differentiation

1 You have something unique – but the customer sees no value in it.
2 You have differentiated too much – more than the customer needs.
3 Your price differentiation is out of proportion to the value of your product.
4 You forgot to create an image – to tell your customers how different you are.
5 You failed to check the real cost of differentiation relative to earnings.
6 Your segmentation was irrelevant, so your differentiation missed its mark.

Steps in a process of differentiation

1 Decide who your customers really are.
2 Sort your customers into groups by demand or buying behaviour.
3 Find out what their buying criteria are – both product related and cosmetic (product mystique).
4 Determine existing and possible ways to offer something unique in terms of those criteria.
5 Determine the costs of existing and potential ways to differentiate.
6 Choose those differentiation variables that give maximum value to the customer in relation to their cost.
7 Test the selected set of variables on your segment of the market.
8 Eliminate costs that have nothing to do with the selected differentiation variables.

Positioning

The concept of positioning, which originated as advertising agency jargon, has attracted growing attention. Lying in the borderland between marketing, portfolio strategy and business strategy, it has sometimes been ultimately decisive to the focusing of corporate resources and thus to the chosen strategic course. Positioning is often a way of getting a competitive edge. Volkswagen in the United States with its 'small is beautiful' slogan, and the Long Island Trust Bank which scored successes by positioning itself as the bank for Long Islanders, are two excellent examples of how positioning helped to create a strategic focus that paved the way to success.

A few words about positioning

The objectives of positioning are:

● to make a company's competence known;
● to inspire better performance;
● to explain a many-faceted complex with organic links;
● to define the place of the company's product in the minds of its customers and other interested parties.

Positioning, then, is something that you do mainly with people, and only secondarily with the product itself.

Positioning further implies expressing yourself in comparative rather than superlative terms. By this I mean that you must relate to the world around you – for example to competitors or other products on the market. It is *not* a matter of trying to endow your product with superlative characteristics and value judgements that other people find artificial and hard to swallow.

An example is Volkswagen's position on the US small-car market. The 'Beetle' was perceived as a *small* car, and was deliberately positioned as such by the message 'small is beautiful'. By taking a position that confirmed a natural impression, Volkswagen automatically gained credibility for its marketing.

Another technique of positioning is to reinforce impressions that already exist in people's minds. The idea is not to change those impressions, but rather to trigger latent associations. You can do this for example by pointing out what you are not: 'Seven-Up – the Non-Cola'.

Positioning involves manipulating people's subjective impressions – finding windows into their minds and associating with something that is already there. It is not so much a matter of creating new mental associations as of confirming existing ones.

Positioning is most closely akin to the concept of image. Image means the way the outside world perceives reality, and is really an expression of what quality means to customers, i.e. how a company is perceived in relation to a set of need-related variables.

Positioning goes a step further: it implies that one is best in a particular segment, i.e. a subset of an area of need or of a total market.

I can cite several examples from my own country. Spendrup, a Swedish brewery, positioned its medium-strength brand as 'premium beer'. The Volvo Car Corporation repositioned itself with the launch of its 700 series, while SAS chose the position of being 'The Businessman's Airline'.

A certain country's largest savings bank was the natural banking contact for all types of business connected with housing. Housing is a central item in the lifetime investment cycles of private persons, so the bank identified housing as the key to its position. By expressing and communicating this position, and by adjusting its range of services accordingly, it succeeded in establishing a strong association in the minds of the general public. That gave it a position on the market which is was then able to exploit for customer relations in a number of areas other than housing.

The concept of positioning is not of course the final answer to all problems of communication and strategy.

Nevertheless it can be an excellent aid to thinking in some cases. You can start with an internal review of what position your company and its products hold in the eyes of the market. From there, in some cases, you can go on to use the terminology of positioning as a focus for strategic orientation and for creation of a competitive edge. Just like 'customer-perceived quality', 'need orientation of product' and similar expressions, the concept of positioning merits a permanent and prominent place in modern management thinking. Figure 19 summarizes the main aspects of positioning.

Fig. 19 Summary of positioning

- Positioning is a carefully considered system for finding a window into people's minds.
- Concentrate on the receiving end. How does the customer perceive my message and my offer?
- Associate with something that is already in people's minds.
- Keep the message simple.
- The easiest and best way to position yourself is to be the first to occupy a particular position.
- Long-term consistency is a very important component of positioning.
- It is often easy to communicate a counter-position (what we are not).
- Never try to position yourself head-on against the market leader.
- The main object of a positioning programme should be to try and claim leadership in a specialized area.
- Find a hole in the market. Where is there a *vacant* leadership position?

Summary of strategy determination

Strategy determination can be considered as the 'halfway house' of the strategy development process. The object of all the work done up to that point – establishment of ambition level, industry and market analyses, portfolio and company analyses and strategy determination – is to decide what course the company should follow. The quality of this work is naturally of great importance. You cannot 'implement' your way to a permanent improvement in your position without careful consideration and a feeling for what you are doing.

Insights beyond the findings of analysis should be added to the process at the strategy determination stage. These insights are derived from business sense, creativity and intuition. While saying this I must emphasize the importance of not relying on intuitive feelings alone: analysis is an essential part of the process. What you need to do is to combine a breakdown of the elements of knowledge, an analysis of these, with mental elasticity and creative reintegration of the elements to arrive at the best possible decision on your future course.

Strategy determination seldom calls for any vast degree of originality; the best thing you can do for your business is often simply to decide which of the available options is preferable and then pursue your chosen course with vigour. In some industries strategy determination involves a fairly uncomplicated choice between a set of options, any one of which is acceptable in itself. The actual making of the choice and the follow-up are then more important than which option is chosen.

In other situations there may be much more riding on the choice you make, especially if it involves committing your company to heavy investment. A shift to market orientation in a service-producing company is usually much less dramatic than in a capital-intensive manufacturing industry. In the latter case, the choice of strategy may well involve investment of such a magnitude as to put the company's survival at risk if the choice proves to be wrong.

Implementation

Introduction

It is the implementation of strategy that has characterized the pattern of success in strategic management which is now beginning to emerge. To those who have been deeply involved in the field of strategy in recent years, implementation stands out as a self-evident and inevitable part of the process. No practical working business executive would agree that theories have any value in themselves: a strategic plan becomes meaningful only when it leads to concrete action, just as only that which one knows really exists. I am therefore assuming that the matter of implementation holds the same fascination for the reader as it does for the author.

The balance between the structural and the dynamic is crucial to successful implementation of changes. The structural part is the actual determination of strategy, i.e. the intellectual foundation of the proposed changes. The dynamic part is the act of making the changes, i.e. the muscle needed to execute the intellectually determined action. Traditional schools of strategy have tended to over-emphasize the intellectual part of the process, whereas in some countries the pendulum has recently swung the other way, with a tendency to deprecate thought and advocate action.

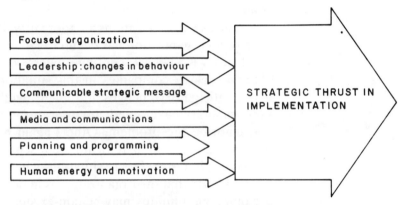

Fig. 20 Implementation of strategy

Strategy development is a powerful tool for raising the level of operational efficiency. We are not discussing here *whether* a chosen strategy should be implemented, but *how* it should be implemented. Implementation is an important part of the concept of strategic *management*, and is the item that distinguishes the latter from strategic *planning*.

- For successful implementation it is necessary to *adapt the organization* to the new strategies.
- *Strong leadership* is needed to teach the strategies, convince people of their value and bring about changes in behaviour.
- There must be a *strategic message* couched in terms that are communicable and meaningful to the target group.
- The *right media* must be chosen for communicating the message.

- All functions of the company must be *programmed* according to the chosen strategies.
- Steps must be taken to develop *human energy and motivation*.

Leadership, energy and communication are the key words in strategy implementation (Fig. 20).

Professors Killing and Fry have presented a structure for change which merits a mention here. The first category of change they call *anticipatory change*. This describes situations where decline and fall are not imminent. In such situations the change is not accepted within the organization. The company continues to thrive regardless, but circumstances in the outside world foreshadow problems to come.

Reactive change situations are those in which the performance of an organization has begun to fall off and the downward trend is likely to continue unless something is done about it. Many companies in this situation have tried to make anticipatory changes and failed, while others in the same category have found glib excuses for explaining away and ignoring the problem. Others again have found it to their advantage to create or inflate a sense of crisis.

Change in crisis refers to situations where it is quite plain to everybody that the organization is in deep trouble. Sales are plunging, liquidity may be non-existent, banks are calling in loans, stockholders are in revolt, etc. Such situations call for fast and resolute action that has a reasonable chance of succeeding.

I am not going into the subject of crisis management here. This section is intended as a guide to strategy implementation in cases where a company still has the option of taking offensive action.

At this point I would like to share some research findings concerning the implementation phase of strategy development. L. Alexander has polled the experience of a large number of heads of companies with regard to the implementation of strategies. The main problems identified by Alexander's survey are listed in Fig. 21.

This list agrees well with my own experience. Too little time and too little resources are devoted to putting the strategy into effect; understanding of the chosen strategies is slower in dawning, and demands a greater educational effort, than had been foreseen. A natural explanation is of course that the people who have participated in formulating

100

Fig. 21 Survey of problems in strategy implementation

Ranking	Problem	% of companies
1	Implementation took longer than originally anticipated	76
2	Major problems arose at the implementation stage that had not been identified beforehand	74
3	Coordination of implementation programmes was not efficient enough	66
4	Other activities and crises prevented management from putting decisions into effect	64
5	Employee competence and ability were inadequate	63
6	Training and instructions for middle management and lower levels were inadequate	62

the strategy tend to underestimate how hard it is for new-comers to grasp what they themselves, after long involve-ment, have come to take for granted. Also, understanding of strategy formulation often demands advanced abstraction capability. That is a quality associated with strategic lead-ership, and not everybody has it.

Organization as a tool of strategy implementation

A company's organization is the most powerful catalyst of change available to it. Change does not itself guarantee progress, but it is axiomatic that there can be no progress without change. The power of organization is omnipotent, and changes sometimes have an intrinsic value in that the educative power of organizational change may be more important than whether the new organizational structure is in fact the optimum one.

Changes in organization are an unexcelled tool for break-ing habitual patterns of behaviour. A change of strategic course should therefore be accompanied by organizational changes that affect most of the people concerned.

The task of a company's organization is to influence demand for the company's products and convert that de-mand into goods and services that match the production apparatus as closely as possible – and to do so with maximum efficiency, i.e. with minimum expenditure of energy.

101

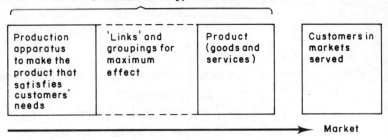

Fig. 22 Task of the organization. The less the weight of the production apparatus, the easier it is to move to the right – towards market orientation

Figure 22 is a graphic representation of this idea, which aims at setting up customer-oriented groupings that will satisfy the whole spectrum of customer needs as efficiently as possible while at the same time being optimally geared to hold the competition at bay. The organization should then strive to swing customer demand gradually towards production and distribution of finished products.

The figure illustrates the importance of a market-orientated approach to investment in production apparatus. Once you have acquired a production apparatus, whether it consists of people or machines, it must pay for itself. The more deeply you commit yourself to a given production apparatus, the harder it is to adapt to the market later on.

When making strategic changes, you may find it useful to ask yourself the following questions about your organization:

- Can we implement our strategies without changing the organization?
- What groupings can deal most effectively with the market?
- What groupings can deal most effectively with the competition?
- What links are needed between the different groupings?
- What supporting systems are needed?
- What problems might arise?

The simplest form of strategy-supporting organization consists of a number of operative divisions corresponding to the business units that exist in the company or group of companies. Each such division or business unit will then contain within itself all, or practically all, the functions and operative decisions it needs to be self-sufficient in the conduct of its operations. In a company with only one business unit, the distinction between company and business unit or division does not apply.

Why, then, is this form of organization so well suited to the purposes of strategic business management?

- It provides a strategic focus on a sector in which unique conditions prevail, so that you can concentrate on being successful in the particular industry in which you are operating without being distracted by considerations that are irrelevant to the business unit.
- Management can be geared to the strategies of the individual business unit and can concentrate on growth, risk assessment, competitive edge and the other elements of strategy.
- Focusing means that you can react more quickly to any threats or opportunities that arise. You are less encumbered by red tape and get a better feeling for the business.
- Rewards can be linked directly to the operating result and balance sheet of the individual profit centre. Morale is higher because it is easier to identify with the strategic position of a business unit than with that of a whole corporation or portfolio.
- Control is much more direct, especially if all functions are contained within the operative division or business unit.

If you set up a divisional structure on business-orientated lines, this often means fragmenting strong staffs and central departments responsible for functions like production, design, marketing, etc., and distributing those departments piecemeal among the new divisions. The managers and personnel of these functional departments naturally find it hard to feel any loyalty to the new, smaller organization. Consequently, a split-up into business units is often sabotaged by strong forces within the organization.

A new business unit should be set up when the criteria for doing so exist. These are:

- a distinct need
- experienced by a defined group of customers
- that can be satisfied by a certain product
- competing with a defined group of other products.

When these conditions are present, the operation needs a specific business strategy. How much autonomy the new division should have is, however, a matter for discussion.

Difficulties arise when circumstances make it uneconomical or impractical to divide a central function among profit-centre divisions. The textbook marketing department of a publishing house can serve as an example: it may not be practical to split this department up between, say, economics and sociology, or between trade sales and mail-order sales.

One way to resolve this problem is to use the 'strategic sector' concept (see p. 37) as a term for groups of business units that are related to each other in at least one respect and therefore ought to share one or more basic functions between them.

> In the data consultancy industry there are several business units in the administrative sector, such as communications, office automation, mainframe computer systems, etc. Each of these units should be allowed to develop professionally on its own, though the needs and customers they serve partly overlap. It may be advantageous for them to have a partly unified marketing organization.

The head of a department that serves more than one master in this way needs to be strongly customer-oriented. If the joint function itself begins to determine the composition of the product it offers to divisions or business units, it robs the heads of those units of their strategic weapons so that they no longer feel responsible for their own development. This is perhaps the commonest drawback to having central functions in divisionalized organizations. The problem is most acute with highly specialized functions like EDP and manufacturing.

A special and frequent problem is that an operation may satisfy the criteria for a business unit, but be so small in relation to other operations that it risks being neglected or rejected. It may have difficulty in paying its share of joint overheads according to corporate cost-sharing principles. Another common situation is that a new operation hatched by the company's R&D department is aimed at entirely new markets and can therefore lay claim to the status of a business unit or division.

One way of handling a small business unit during its growth to maturity is to make it part of another unit, which will thus be *in loco parentis* to the smaller one. Another way is to let the unit make its own way outside the parent culture and thereby improve its chances of survival.

In cases where you want to get a strategic focus on a certain group of products but fragmentation into business units is not appropriate or possible, one way out is to appoint

104

product managers. By doing so, however, you lose some of the advantages mentioned above.

The head office or group management function can be discussed on a basis of staffs or of the management's vital interest in having units that are successful though independent. We will not dwell here on the question of staffs, but simply list in point form the most essential and legitimate tasks of a group management with a number of autonomous profit centres under its umbrella.

```
┌─────── Organize on the basis of goals and strategies ────────┐
│                        with a view to                        │
│ • creating a business-oriented company that satisfies and develops │
│   certain market needs                                        │
│ • creating a result-oriented, self-sufficient organization in │
│   which different business areas can be independently optimized │
│ • refining the production apparatus with reference to market  │
│   development and products                                    │
│ • creating management resources capable of working towards    │
│   defined overriding goals on their own initiative            │
│ • laying down clear and well-defined areas of responsibility for │
│   maximum delegation leading to fast reactions, higher motivation │
│   and the shortest possible decision-making channels          │
└──────────────────────────────────────────────────────────────┘
```

Fig. 23 Purpose of organization in the strategy development process

Top management should:

- appoint competent managers to implement its strategy;
- set up control systems to give early warning of any problem in any unit;
- ensure that a credible strategy is formulated, and that this strategy is compatible with group goals;
- intervene decisively if necessary, even if this upsets the head of the business unit concerned;
- reward excellent unit managers and replace bad ones;
- act as a strategic sparring partner or sounding board for unit management;
- approve major transactions of a structural nature.

The timing of organizational changes prompted by new strategies should be announced at the same time as the strategies themselves are presented. Quick action emphasizes that management means business with its new strategies, and new allocations of responsibility encourage people to devote their best energies to implementing the new strategies.

Organization is a matter of differentiation and integration. A differentiation based on a division into business units may show encouraging results in the short term, but be counterproductive to the long-term development of the company, whether its portfolio is synergic or diversified. The balance between differentiation and integration is therefore a key issue that needs very careful consideration in each individual case.

Leadership and changes in behaviour

The primary task of management is to ensure that a company's operations are continually adapted, rationalized and reoriented in response to changes in its environment, and that the adaptations are made with optimum resource utilization and with the wholehearted cooperation of employees. Some situations, specifically strategic reorientations, make much heavier demands on leadership skills than do more gradual changes.

There are many definitions of leadership. I have chosen to list below some characteristics cited as criteria of good leadership by some people with management experience. According to them a leader should be:

open and extroverted	calm
inquisitive	quick to understand
sensitive	warm and empathetic
result oriented	unbound by prestige
decisive	courageous
critical	capable of bringing out
ready to experiment and	the best in others
tolerate mistakes	a good listener
confidence-inspiring	unflappable
charismatic and	flexible
enthusiasm inspiring	

Leadership as applied to strategy implementation has four chief aims:

● to make the strategies *known*;
● to encourage *positive attitudes* and commitment to the strategies;
● to *motivate people to act* in support of the strategies;
● to *get the organization moving* and make sure the strategies are put into effect.

No change can be successfully made unless the people in the organization are conscious of the need for change. A

106

leader responsible for implementing a process of change must be able to *convince* the people around him that the chosen course is the right one. Individuals have a tendency to defend the status quo to an extent that makes the progress of change far too sluggish.

To get a strategy implemented, a strong leader must convince all his listeners that the chosen course is the only right one, and the one that will lead to a more trouble-free future. A strong and convinced top management that has participated in the process is essential to successful implementation. The mangement itself must also be prepared to make an extraordinary effort, no matter how many consultants it has engaged to help with the process of implementation.

In the Western world, the instinct to obey has gradually atrophied to the point where it is no longer realistic to expect uncritical acceptance of new policies. On the contrary, the basic reaction is more likely to be critical or negative.

Top management as a body must be involved in the process of strategy determination, but even so it cannot be safely assumed that all its members are wholly sold on the new strategies or will automatically act in accordance with them. I have seen examples of passive acceptance being transformed into active obstruction as soon as the people concerned were removed from the power centre of strategy determination.

To implement your strategy, then, you must be able to convince the people around you, and you must also be skilled in social theatre. To be convincing, you need the attributes of a good and forceful teacher. Management must be able to show why it chose the strategy it did rather than any of the other possible alternatives. This calls not only for stringent logic in the analysis and the message, but also for persuasiveness and the ability to win over the waverers to your side.

Information and communication are key words in the teaching process. The trouble with information is the same as with love and money – people never feel they are getting enough. Management must learn to live with the fact that nobody ever thinks that they have been given enough information. People want information because there is status in having it, preferably more of it than others have.

Beware, however, of letting a copious flow of information be a substitute for leadership in the strategy development process. Education must be staged according to who is getting it. The idea is that the new strategies should have a concrete effect on the work of every individual, so the educational process should be so designed that all employees are informed and led in such a way as to guide their behaviour in their respective jobs.

You should perhaps pay special attention to people on the middle management level, whose authority is often founded on hierarchical tradition. They may feel their position threatened by strategy development processes in which their subordinates suddenly acquire a high level of knowledge of corporate policy.

The inertia that one encounters when trying to implement a strategy is a perfectly normal phenomenon. There are always long-standing traditional patterns of behaviour for all routines – buying materials, invoicing customers, geting paid for overtime, holding executive conferences and all kinds of other activities. The channels of communication are well known and worn smooth. Actions and attitudes have become hallowed with time.

One of the first tactical moves in strategy implementation is a thorough review of all existing routines, policies and methods in the light of the new strategies. This review should cover both official and informal norms and routines. Revised norms and routines should be worked out to reflect the new strategies, and introduced as part of the behaviour pattern and culture of the new organization.

In addition to the more formal routines and policies, you will need to adjust the whole complex of informal behaviour implied by the term 'corporate culture'. A period of personal interpretation, experimentation, practice and improvision will be needed to work out new patterns of behaviour to fit the new strategies. A change in strategy will not be fully effective until the adjustments have had time to take hold. Figure 24 illustrates how psychological factors are changed over a period of time by changes in strategy.

Every established organization has its own culture. This is a vogue word for a set of attitudes to things like dealing with customers, spending money, taking risks, taking initiative and many others. Here the old saying that people do what you do instead of what you tell them to do applies with full force. In other words, the power of example is an important part of strategy implementation. It takes a lot of time and effort to get employees to understand and apply new rules for behaviour, and inducements must be constructed to encourage them to change their ways. Many leaders have

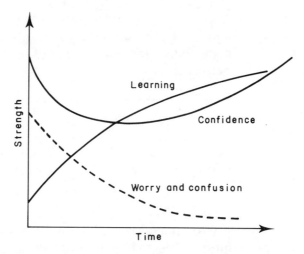

Fig. 24 Psychological factors related to system changes. The graph shows how reactions to change alter with time. (Freely adapted from Newman, W.H., The Process of Management, *Prentice-Hall 1982.)*

discovered that they have underestimated the difficulty of bringing about a change in strategy by failing to realize just how time-consuming and repetitive this process is.

The choice of the right leaders is perhaps the most crucial of all issues connected with strategy implementation. This applies not only to the chief executive, but also to the rest of the management team entrusted with the task.

When considering the choice of leadership, it helps to ask three questions:

● What kind of leader is best fitted to implement the chosen strategies?
● Do the present top men have what it takes, or can they adapt to acquire what it takes?
● To what extent would the company benefit from new leadership?

I shall not go into detail here about choice of leaders. Experience shows that strategic change can generally be accomplished much more easily and quickly with an all-new top management team, as this gets away from all the vested interests, bonds of friendship and prestige that often interfere with the efficiency of the process.

How to reward strategic skills is a crucial issue of leadership. All businesses reward operative skills according to some kind of result-related yardstick, which is both necessary and desirable. The difficulty lies in also rewarding

109

strategic skills that may not show results until several years after they have been applied. The time span depends on the nature of the business; it is shortest in service-producing companies. Here are some hints on how to reward strategic performance:

- Measure progress towards strategic goals separately from operative results.
- Establish rewards for strategic progress separately from rewards for short-term operative success.
- If possible, set up stock bonus and stock option schemes in such a way as to encourage strategic management, entrepreneurship and risk-taking.

Experiments have been made in many countries whereby future rights to buy stock on advantageous terms are linked to the development of a company over an extended period of time. Whether or not the leader stays with the company, he is encouraged to take the long view and think strategically during his time with it.

The strategic reward situation can be likened to that of the forester planting trees that will not yield timber in his lifetime, or of the nuclear-powered icebreaker salesman who may have to work for no return for years before he finally makes a sale.

In my opinion it is advisable to spend much more time than you originally reckoned with on securing the support of your trade unions. Realization of the need to get a decent return on invested capital is more widespread among unions in some countries than others. In Sweden, recognition of ROI as a yardstick justifying a company's existence has now gone so far in union circles that there are normally no insurmountable difficulties in putting through a change that will benefit the company. In other countries the situation is different, but this is nearly always due to lack of information and education about the facts of business life. It is true that one sometimes encounters sheer stupidity or open hostility, but those are exceptional cases. The necessary effort must therefore be made on a fairly basic level – something that is apt to be forgotten by people accustomed to operating on the Olympian heights of management.

The strategy message

In the foregoing section we considered the question of who should be involved in shaping a new strategic course. That naturally includes all employees, but divided into target groups according to each group's need to know about the new policies.

The second important need is to formulate the strategy message in comprehensible terms. At one extreme, you can draft a 20- or 40-page document that deals in detail with each and every one of the elements or expressions of strategy. At the other extreme, you can coin a pithy motto like 'Businessman's Airline' or 'Management Data Consultants' that simply and concisely captures the essence of your company's strategic aims. Between those extremes there will be a need to express and adapt the strategy message in a variety of ways for different target groups, and to communicate it through a variety of media.

A full-dress strategy should be presented in the form of the nine elements of strategy:

1. *corporate mission* expressed in terms of needs, product, customers and competitors;
2. *competitive edge* explaining how the company is going to compete more successfully on its market;
3. *business organization* describing businesses, products and markets and how the organization will be differentiated and integrated;
4. *product* in the form of goods and services optimally adapted to satisfying customers' needs;
5. *development programmes* for businesses, products and markets;
6. *acquisition and discontinuation* of units to mark structural changes;
7. *resources* showing how strategies will be supported by investment in machinery and buildings, but also by build-up of know-how and other cost allocations;
8. *management competence and culture* expressed in terms of appointments to various executive positions and presentation of ideas to be nurtured or introduced;
9. *markets* as a statement of which customers the company most wants to do business with.

Obviously you cannot expound every element of strategy in detail. If for example your plans call for dropping a business unit, you must be very careful to avoid spreading alarm and despondency in that unit.

One suggestion is that you divide everybody concerned into target groups according to how much detailed information about the strategic course each group ought to be given.

Then you can draft an outline for your strategy message, and give it to a competent firm of communication experts to work up into easily assimilable messages.

A message that is too smooth and superficial will be regarded by skilled professional people as something of an insult to their intelligence, while a message that is too complicated and too detailed for its target group will be rejected.

Latter-day strategy messages have sometimes tended to take on a rhetorical tone that gives an impression of being cosmetic. Popularized slogans like 'The customer is the most important person in our business' are too vague, although they may of course be deeply relevant to certain industries. The main thing is too keep the gap between rhetoric and realism as narrow as possible.

The media of strategy

The function of a medium is to transmit a message as efficiently as possible. When the subject is a new strategic course, the maxim that 'the medium is the message' is truer than otherwise: management's ability to communicate its message is of paramount importance. If management doubts its ability to get its message across with the necessary impact, it must of course choose other media. The most important medium is person-to-person communication, but there are many other channels:

- group briefings
- seminars
- information sheets
- official documentation
- training courses
- discussions in local trade union branches
- audiovisual shows
- speeches on festive occasions
- articles in the press

The list could be made longer. Staged educational programmes are proven by experience to be a tremendously effective medium, though they are seldom used for such purposes. By letting a professional training institute train picked people in your organization to go out and train the rest, you can go a long way to winning widespread understanding of your strategic aims.

Functional strategic orientation

One essential step in strategy implementation is getting the various functions into line with the new strategic aims of the business unit. Here, as before, the term 'functions' refers to departments like R&D, manufacturing, EDP, marketing, administration, personnel, etc. The managers of these functions must be induced to devote all their energies to recasting their respective areas of responsibility in the new strategic mould.

Unexpectedly often one finds that people who have attended meetings about a new strategic course come away without understanding that course, even though it may seem perfectly clear to the people who have taken part in the process of plotting it. One frequent manifestation of this is that people go out and do things that take them in a diametrically opposite direction. In short, it is easy to underestimate the need for a process of learning and indoctrination, even for executives with quite extensive areas of responsibility.

The company management should of course have a clear idea of how the unit's various functions ought to be reoriented in the light of the new strategies. It is a common observation that the functions farthest from the business end always find it hardest to fall into line with new strategies. Control systems, for example, invariably lag behind in the process of change. Another function that always seems to carry on as if nothing had happened is personnel. Personnel functions are often headed by competent people schooled under the 'old paradigm' of administrative management. Only in exceptional cases has the latter-day swing to entrepreneurship and business orientation made itself felt in personnel departments.

By making functional managers responsible for adapting their functional strategies to the overall business strategy, you get an automatic check on how far the new strategies have been accepted and understood.

Planning and programming have become indispensable tools for assuring the realization of strategies. The 'old' role of the planning technocrats as controllers of strategy has thus changed. Unfortunately, many companies have neglected to use the planning tool and have overestimated the self-propulsive force of the process of change once the intellectual work is done. One reason for this neglect may be the excessive faith that the old paradigm placed in planning as an instrument of change – which has helped to consign planning to the doghouse.

Planning in this context means systematic work at functional level designed to change the orientation of the function and bring it into line with the new business strategies. This work should lead to concrete changes and reappraisals of existing resource allocations and goals for the work of all organizational units in the *new* organization built up after the change in strategy.

Planning comprises a set of functional goals and strategies for reaching those goals within a given time horizon dimensioned according to the nature of the business and the time horizons of the business strategies.

Programming comprises the concrete steps that must be taken under the new functional strategies starting immediately. Programming is decisive in giving the push to start things rolling.

The basic components in the construction of a programme are universally applicable:

A Divide the project into steps or phases.
B Divide each step into chronological sequences.
C Allocate responsibility for each step.
D Establish resources and availability for each step.
E Work out how much time will be needed for each step.
F Set starting and completion dates for each step based on A, B, D and E.

The amount of detail and the scope of the programming exercise will depend on the needs of the situation. Those needs will depend in turn on the type of project to be put into effect, and on the nature of the business and the characters of the individuals responsible for doing the job.

Fully programmed projects are almost endlessly detailed. The classic example is NASA's 'Man on the Moon' project, in which every component and activity was programmed according to a new methodology.

A technique that is generally better suited to the purposes of strategy is to advance step by step, feeling your way. The degree of uncertainty is generally so great that adjustments must and should be made as the implementation of the new strategy takes shape. Uncertainty is in fact often one of the hallmarks of strategy. Even the first estimates of earnings, costs and use of resources contain uncertainties and probabilities that will cause deviations from the original plans.

The making of plans and the initiation of programmes for

implementation of new strategies are however decisive factors for the success of strategy development. It is quite justifiable to err a little on the side of detail in order to be sure that plans are made and programmes started. In these respects modern strategic management displays a close kinship with old-time strategic planning, though generally on a more realistic plane and with much greater energy and likelihood of accomplishment.

Though planning is of decisive importance, it differs in kind from the old-style 'strategic plan'. Modern strategy techniques use the planning function as an important means of strategy implementation. Under the old system, planning technocracy came to be an end in itself instead of a means to an end. I am not denigrating the planning function – just insisting that it be kept in its proper perspective.

The biggest real-life difficulty in the implementation of new strategies is the collision with ongoing business operations. Strategic change upsets the balance of smoothworn routines and is therefore viewed with disfavour by many of the people caught up in it. Strategy implementation requires a high level of initiative, energy and imagination to overcome instinctive defence of the status quo.

Even well-prepared programmes can run into trouble when the time comes to put them into effect; there is a tendency to shove them into the background. A structure that is balanced and dimensioned for existing operative needs possesses an inertia that can easily stifle new programmes fumbling their way towards radical change.

Human resources

HRM *(human resource management)* is becoming an increasingly important part of strategy development processes. As companies' primary products (the basic goods and services they offer) grow more and more alike, the key to success must be sought ever farther away among the 'soft' variables, which are overwhelmingly influenced and shaped by people. As we have already seen, a shift is now taking place in the direction of more decisiveness, initiative, drive and creativity. As a result of the complexity of business life, confidence in risk-minimizing studies has declined. Trial and error is being used to an incresing extent as an instrument for testing new business ideas without ruinous risk.

The question of how to release indwelling human energy

has thus become a crucial issue of strategy. The little research that has been done on the quality concept shows that the importance which customers attach to the service component when choosing their suppliers is much greater than the people employed in supplying companies realize. The latter tend to overrate the importance of the basic service in comparison with peripheral services. Sheet metal manufacturers, for example, pay too much attention to metallurgy and tolerances and too little to delivery times, customer care and the quality of their sales effort.

People, then, are becoming an ever more important competitive factor. This applies, according to research done in the PIMS database, to *all* industries, regardless of what kind of goods or services they supply.

HRM is an integral part of the strategy process, and one that ought to be activated. Otherwise there is a great danger that this important function will be handled on habitual lines by a traditional personnel department. There is a great danger that selection, promotion, inducements and motivation will proceed just as before and that certain kinds of knowledge and skill will be emphasized just as before. Strategic realignment is possibly more important for the function responsible for HRM than for any other.

A few key questions with regard to HRM in the strategic context:

● How can we utilize the human resource as a force for change?
● What excellent and unique human resources that ought to be cultivated do we have in our company?
● What human resources are lacking and need to be added to reach our new strategic goals?
● What human resources are likely to be in short supply in our industry in the future?
● Can we find mutually beneficial ways of using people who are not capable of handling the responsibilities they have?

Possibly the greatest potential, however, lies in increasing the energy output of the existing human resource. This can be accomplished through greater movitation, which in turn depends on a clearly marked will to change things in a direction that a great majority of the personnel accept as desirable.

Individuals in a company should no longer be regarded as costs for cutting, but as a powerful instrument for making the process of change effective.

116

Some advice on implementation of strategies

Perhaps the most important basic piece of advice is that you must be prepared to generate all the energy needed to bring about a successful change. General experience confirms that the initial effort was never as determined as hindsight shows it ought to have been to achieve full success. By all means enlist outside help in the form of consultants, not just in the analysis and strategy determination stages but perhaps above all as catalysts in the implementation stage. A catalyst is an individual who makes a process run faster and more easily without actually taking part in it. Even people inside the company can act as catalysts. Give every manager the tools and opportunities to analyse his own situation – eye-openers are needed.

- Use and refer to a good analysis of your industry and market, or other analyses or parts thereof that can help to make your organization more ready to accept change.
- Make a list of the prejudices, objections and arguments for maintaining the status quo that you encounter in your organization.
- In my company, Indevo, we speak of the 20–60–20 rule, according to which 20% are spontaneously in favour of change, 60% are indifferent and 20% are opposed. You need to get the uncommitted 60% on your side to win over the organization for change.
- Activate line managers on all levels in the company to make them take a creative approach to their own areas of responsibility and thereby help to further the strategy development process. Contact the unions, too, at an early stage in the proceedings and keep them informed throughout the process.
- Make changes in organization and management as necessary. Avoid leaving the same old monkeys up the same old trees. Renew both the organization and the management structure, otherwise people may not realize that a change is in progress.
- Keep up a fast pace, if necessary at the expense of precision. But time the spurt carefully; don't gallop away until you have recruited enough people in management positions as enthusiastic and committed members of your team.
- Try to distinguish between structural problems and bad management. It is too easy to condemn somebody trying to run an operation from a hopeless strategic position.

● As soon as a new organization is decided on, make a concentrated effort to establish follow-up systems that fit the new organization.

These are a few examples of the pitfalls to avoid and the signposts to follow along a new strategic road. Talk to other people with first-hand experience of this kind of process. There are not many of them, but their know-how is valuable.

5 Strategies for business development

Introduction and definition

The contents of this book are generally applicable to strategic processes regardless of a company's current situation. The reasons why I have included a chapter on strategies for business development are that the subject is topical at the time of writing and that it has received relatively little attention in the traditional practice of strategy. As we have seen, the older schools of strategy were mainly concerned with experience curves, production efficiency and economies of scale. I therefore wanted to take advantage of experience from business development processes and explain some of the commonest approaches and techniques.

Fig. 25 Business development

---

* Increases volume of operations
* Generates outward-dressing energy
* Creates business
* Needs – product – creativity – quality

Figure 25 summarizes what I mean by business development under a few brief headings. Business development contributes to *increasing the volume of operations*. This refers to a series of actions, aimed at profitability rather than cost reduction, with the ultimate aim of expanding a company's operations – which must of course remain profitable in the long term. Business development may, however, just like any other forward-looking programme such as an upgrading of quality, have a short-term negative effect on profitability.

Another aim of business development is to vitalize the existing main business and to increase the flow of outward-directed energy at the expense of internal energy consumption. I resort to these somewhat grandiose expressions after having observed a number of organizations which, as they grew, began to expend more and more energy on maintaining and preserving the basic organization itself. Internal conferences, making adjustments to production apparatus and personnel, a constant growth of the need for internal communications, etc., make it all too easy to forget about customers and to use up more and more energy on inward things. This is one of the main reasons why companies lose their ability to compete. The increasing internal energy consumption is unfortunately accompanied by dwindling alertness to the changing pattern of customers' needs.

To put it in a nutshell, business development creates business instead of administering business that somebody else has created. Those of us who studied business management at college were mainly taught techniques for managing companies created by others. This of course is an important and necessary skill, but it is equally true that it is not enough to administer the status quo: old operations need to be reshaped and new ones started in order to keep the wheels of business turning.

The business development concept has come to symbolize a combination of entrepeneurship, which is the hallmark of performance-motivated individuals who are willing to take risks, with systematic strategy development focused on vitalizing the revenue-generating side of business. The business development concept has been beneficial to management culture and deserves a permanent place among the tenets of managerial science. Otherwise there is a danger that phenomena like business development will be dismissed as mere passing fads.

Business development is concerned with essentials like needs and the verification of needs, with creativity in the sense of ability to combine known elements of knowlege in new and innovative ways, with product renewal and with ways to enhance quality as perceived by the customer. I shall return to these matters below.

The strategic umbrella of business development

Figure 26 shows a way of classifying the structure of business development that will be used in the rest of this chapter.

Under the umbrella we find two main concepts: organic growth, and diversification. A closer study reveals that there is no sharp dividing line. Organic growth refers to development of business on the basis of skills or assets that already exist for the most part, while diversification refers to operations that bear little or no relation to the original business.

Going from left to right in the figure we move from a situation most closely resembling the present one to business operations that differ maximally from what we are doing today. This visualization lays no claim to strict scientific rigour, but it has proved a useful aid to discussion of ways and means to vitalize the revenue-generating side of companies' operations.

Vitalization of existing principal business

If we want to produce a short-term improvement in operating results, we must of course take measures of the kind that quickly bring down total costs, such as:

- shutting down
- slimming down
- renegotiating
- boosting productivity
- releasing tied-up capital

Thus when we talk about vitalizing existing principal business, we are talking about companies that have enough survival force to be able to turn their attention to the question of development. This is an important distinction, as one might otherwise be tempted to suppose that development is the cure for all ills. Such is not the case: there must be a stable platform to provide the focus for survival. There are three effective ways of vitalizing a principal business operation: I shall now deal with them in turn.

Create strategic clarity

Performing a strategic audit is a valuable way of clarifying your own thinking on what your company's strategies are

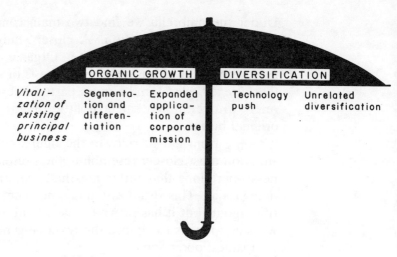

ORGANIC GROWTH			DIVERSIFICATION	
Vitali- zation of existing principal business	Segmenta- tion and differen- tiation	Expanded applica- tion of corporate mission	Technology push	Unrelated diversification

Fig. 26a The strategic umbrella of business development

and whether the various functions in the company are truly aligned with the prevailing strategies. By reviewing the elements of strategy – corporate mission, product, competitive edge, market, business organization, resources, structural changes, management style/culture and development programme – you can get an idea of what strategies are actually in force. Having determined this, you can check how well the various functions are aligned with those strategies.

Having studied the collective direction of thrust of your strategies, you can take a look at how well the strategies are communicated and how far they inspire people to bend their efforts in a given direction. You might find a lack of clarity about strategies, in which case your next obvious step is to try and establish clarity. By putting special emphasis on business, market and product development, you can indicate the business development character of the process.

The creation of strategic clarity will usually bring about a higher level of energy and, by the same token, a vitalization of your business operations.

Adapt product to needs

It ought to go without saying that a company's range of products and services should be adapted to the structure of needs on its market. I have gradually come to understand why a discrepancy so often exists.

Newly started companies are always marketing-oriented and customer-focused because they must get very close to the customer and his needs in order to survive at all. But as the organization grows, the focus of its interest and energy gradually drifts to other things than markets and customers. It begins to concern itself with its production apparatus and its personnel. These are legitimate concerns in themselves: the trouble is that if you spend too much time on them, you can easily lose touch with what is going on in the marketplace. Poor competitive performance in a principal area of business is directly attributable to a mismatch between product and needs. Though the underlying need structures are fairly constant, demand is not static: it changes all the time. It is easy to lose sight of which way demand is moving, but if that happens your sales wil start to fall off.

Understanding the structure of customers' needs makes your company better able to adjust its product to those needs and thereby steer customer demand to its own product.

Customers, like voters, are characterized by a high degree of inertia. They go on buying the same old product, just as they go on voting for the same old party, long after the alternative has in fact shown itself to be better. This gives a big company a substantial advantage, in that it has plenty of time to renew its product provided that it is sensitive to early warnings.

Need studies of various kinds have therefore become increasingly popular. PDS (problem detection studies) and similar techniques are a good way to find out what problems customers experience in using existing products and services. Image may be a decisive factor in know-how-intensive companies, and there are also other need-related concepts like customer-perceived quality that could bear investigation.

Making a correct appraisal of the structure of needs is one of the most difficult things to do. Do people buy shoes to keep their feet warm, or to express their egos and personalities, or are their motives mixed?

A good example of this difficulty is the hyper-rational attitude exhibited by the head of a large car manufacturing company at the beginning of the 1970s. What he said, roughly, was that a car should be a safe and reliable means of transportation and that fripperies like horsepower and so on were entirely secondary to the need for reliable transportation. His mistake was a common one: he assumed that his customers were just as rationally minded as he was, and so grossly misjudged the true structure of needs on his market (see my earlier remarks on the rationality trap). Today everybody knows that the choice of a car is an expression of personality, individuality, status, etc. This is all the more true because the primary need, i.e. for safe and rational transportation, can be satisfied by all the brands on the market and is therefore only a marginal product-differentiating factor.

Marketing audit

The term 'marketing audit' refers to a way of thinking rather than to a fully developed model. It simply means questioning and reconsidering the resources used primarily for revenue-generating purposes, or in other words the marketing function. A marketing audit must be conducted by somebody outside the organization. In principle it involves a kind of zero-base approach: if there were no marketing organization at all, how ought one to be constructed?

You may find it hard to believe that there are sales forces which are not controlled by sales performance, and big advertising budgets that are spent without reference to results (I am not of course referring to institutional advertising). I have known companies where it would have been perfectly easy to measure this performance of individual salespeople but where no attempt was made to do so, much less to set up inducements that would have encouraged more effective selling. This may be attributable partly to poor sales management and partly to some exaggerated gerrymandering of customers in an attempt to ensure 'fair shares'.

The marketing audit technique has been described elsewhere, so I will not dwell upon it here. The important thing is to understand the idea, which is that allocation of resources to the marketing function ought to be questioned and, if necessary, radically revised. An understanding of what customers need and what makes them tick is fundamental to this exercise. It calls for great breadth of thought to make a correct diagnosis of a company's marketing needs.

Segmentation and differentiation

I have dealt elsewhere with the art of segmenting the market correctly. Customers' needs are the only proper basis for

124

segmentation. Geographical areas, age-groups, sizes of companies, etc. are only approximations of customer needs and of the structure of demand.

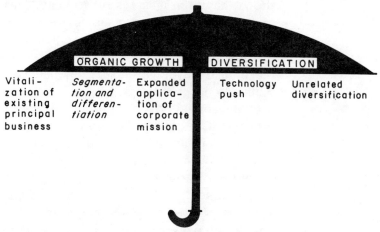

Fig. 26b The strategic umbrella of business development

Segmentation and differentiation simply mean that you carefully review the need structures of customers and divide your customers into segments to get a basis for differentiating your product and thereby hopefully achieve a level of profitability above the average for your industry.

A niche was formerly defined as a segment in which the pressure of competition is less than in the market as a whole. It is conceivable for a company both to operate in niches in order to make itself more competitive in one segment of the market and earn more money, and to divide the total market into segments and differentiate its product with reference to the market as a whole.

An example from the automotive industry is illuminating. General Motors can safely be assumed to want to differentiate its product to appeal on the whole market, except possibly the extreme top and bottom ends. General Motors was actually on the point of wiping out Ford at the beginning of the 1930s when it discovered the blessings of differentiation as opposed to Ford's economy-of-scale philosophy symbolized by the black Model T. The drawbacks to this strategy are equally obvious. GM has difficulty in projecting the exclusiveness in certain segments enjoyed by Mercedes Benz, BMW, Volvo and Saab, just because those brands are not mass products and are not represented in many of the other segments.

In contrast to GM's strategy, BMW stands out as a 'niche' company that has chosen its own strategic focus. This means it has picked out a niche in the market and concentrated on that niche to improve its profitability – which, the record shows, has been a successful strategy. This is an excellent example of positioning, a subject we covered in Chapter 4.

The aim of differentiation is to enhance the uniqueness of the product, i.e. to offer goods and services that differ from the industry average and better match the needs of the segment concerned.

One essential effect of product differentiation is the improvement in quality that sometimes accompanies such a strategy. Upward qualitative differentiation generally leads to an improvement in the whole organization, which helps to make it more profitable.

A parallel can suitably be drawn with the theory of strategic groups. The automotive industry also illustrates how a company can upgrade its competitive position by moving from one strategic group to another. BMW did just that a long time ago, and both Volvo and Saab in Sweden are now following suit. Volvo, with the launch of its 700 series, has moved closer to Mercedes, while Saab with its 9000 Turbo 16 has moved closer to BMW. The reason why I use cars as examples is that they are so well known, but the argument applies equally to many other industries. The important thing is to correctly diagnose the needs that are the criteria for market segmentation.

When we speak of differentiation we are inclined to think in terms of upgrading, but there are examples of the opposite. People Express is a case in point. I also know of an insurance company in a country in Western Europe which plans to drop a whole array of marginal insurance services that have been tacked on to traditional household insurance policies. That way they can substantially reduce the premium for the basic policy while letting the customer decide for himself whether he wants any optional extra coverage. In strategy literature, this is called 'unbundling'.

Expanded application of corporate mission

A company's corporate mission applies to a certain market that it serves. This means that it supplies customers

126

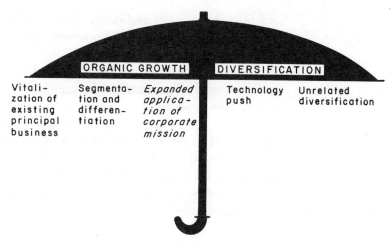

ORGANIC GROWTH			DIVERSIFICATION	
Vitali- zation of existing principal business	Segmenta- tion and differen- tiation	*Expanded* *applica-* *tion of* *corporate* *mission*	Technology push	Unrelated diversification

Fig. 26c   The strategic umbrella of business development

of a certain kind with good or services that satisfy their needs.

According to the classic product/market matrix, we can imagine a company broadening its corporate mission to embrace a wider range of needs and/or a wider circle of customers.

To put it in more concrete terms, a Belgian company could consider selling its products in Holland too, or a company that sells ships' propellers might consider adding electronic steering systems to its range.

Whether you find new geographical markets, new applications or new products to add to your range, the new additions should have some kinship in the structure of customers' needs. A shipyard buys ships' propellers, but also kitchen chairs and airplane tickets. There is sometimes an exaggerated belief in synergies based on the fallacy that an industrial customer is a monolith.

The term 'market' is a slippery one: it can be used in either a geographical or a transactional sense, which can sometimes confuse the issues.

When considering any addition to your product range, you should proceed from the areas of need you are satisfying now. With reference to those areas of need you should check thoroughly that the structure of purchasing actually matches the area of need you have identified. An industrial customer seldom buys airplane tickets and propellers through the same channel. A private person, on the other hand, is a monolith in terms of buying, though of course preferences naturally vary between individuals. Internationalization, vertical integration and other traditional key concepts are expressions of the strategy known as 'broadening the corporate mission'.

It is easy to find examples of how concentration to fewer areas of operation, combined with broadening and internationalization within those areas, has proved to be a successful stratey. It has been particularly successful for companies with small home markets – like Sweden for example. Saab-Scania, Swedish Match and the Bahco Group are a few examples of Swedish companies which at different times have simultaneously concentrated and internationalized their operations.

Technology push

I have chosen to deal with technology push under a separate heading because it is such an important factor in industrial growth. Many products and services have seen the light of day as a result of pure technological fervour and tinkering. They have subsequently helped to reinforce the foundations of commerce.

The reason why I have classed technology push under diversification is that the commercial character of new technological advances often differs widely from their originators' basic line of business. If jet engine combustion yields spin-off in the form of car heaters or incinerators for destruction of noxious gases, the commercial connection is non-existent.

The principal strategy is a matter of exploiting a technological base in new business areas. In this situation everything is new, except the technology and maybe the production apparatus. One example is the sensational drug Healon, made by the Swedish Pharmacia company, which is now used both to treat horses' knee joints and as an aid to complicated eye surgery.

Some researchers in the 1970s began to study the emergence of new technology-based business operations. Unfortunately the failure rate among such businesses has been extremely high, and the probability of success in any individual case is dauntingly small. The main reasons for these depressing statistics are to be sought not in faulty technology, but in the difficulty of bridging the gap between engineering development and business development.

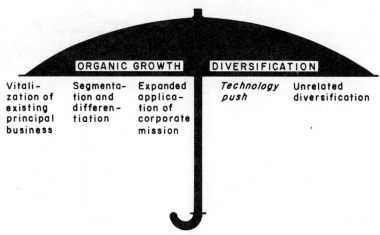

ORGANIC GROWTH			DIVERSIFICATION	
Vitali-zation of existing principal business	Segmenta-tion and differen-tiation	Expanded applica-tion of corporate mission	*Technology push*	Unrelated diversification

Fig. 26d The strategic umbrella of business development

If you can inject business development skills into technologically strong companies and get access to know-how and research in the field concerned, the individual company stands to gain a lot.

Technology, in the widest sense of the word, is also an important growth factor in service-producing companies. Their accumulated fund of know-how or system structure can often provide a basis for corporate missions that involve exploitation of available resources in other business areas.

A business operation arising out of technology push does not necessarily have to be carried on by the parent company itself. You can consider licensing, selling or collaborating with other companies who know the market in the relevant field. A technology often has applications in a number of industries, so the company that wants to exploit the technology must carefully consider what strategies it is going to adopt for each industry. This is one of the more difficult problems that arise in business development.

A packaging company had mastered extrusion technology. It had diversified itself by setting up a consumer division that sold wrapping paper, carrier bags and a number of other associated products. The extrusion technique was also applicable to the manufacture of pipework insulation, sanitary pads and ID cards. The business strategy problem, then, was to decide which basic strategy to adopt for operations in each of these areas. At one end of the scale they could start an in-house operation, as in the case of the consumer division, and at the other they could become suppliers of intermediates or sell the developed intermediate technology.

129

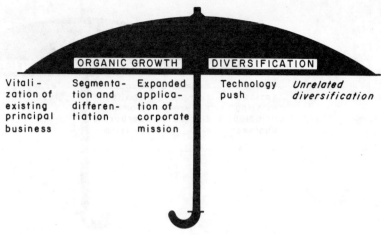

ORGANIC GROWTH			DIVERSIFICATION	
Vitali- zation of existing principal business	Segmenta- tion and differen- tiation	Expanded applica- tion of corporate mission	Technology push	*Unrelated diversification*

Fig. 26e The strategic umbrella of business development

Unrelated diversification

Diversification was quite fashionable during the 1960s and early 1970s. The theory behind it was that there existed a universal type of management skill which meant that if you were running your present company successfully, you could run any company successfully. Diversification later fell somewhat into disrepute on account of the many failures it led to. Latter-day insights have revealed that a lot more is involved than general management skill.

There are three basic motives for adopting a strategy based on unrelated diversification: overliquidity, an eroding corporate mission, and a desire to spread risks.

Overliquidity

A company that is profitable in its own field of operations, but which for one reason or another cannot expand its corporate mission to encompass new products and new markets, has no choice but to diversify. The situations I have described may seem hypothetical, but it does arise some-times. One case in point was a company that held agency rights in a certain territory where it had captured the lion's share of the market. There was no way that market could be expanded, and customers' needs in that area were already satisfied, so the only road to further expansion was through diversification.

130

Eroding corporate mission

There are circumstances in which the very foundations of your business can be cut away so that you are forced to do something else. The classic case, of course, is that of buggy-whip makers at the dawn of the automobile age.

We can speak of 'strategic black holes' in which strategy development on normal premises is impossible and you have to resort to some radical measure like cashing in your assets and investing the money in something entirely different. Corporate missions, like political philosophies, are related to a certain period in time and must sooner or later die or change out of all recognition. In such situations, capital is the only link between the old business and the new.

Spreading risks

Suppose the party in power in a small country regularly passed resolutions at its annual party congresses calling for the nationalization of the drug industry. It would be quite natural for the owner of a successful pharmaceutical house in that country to start thinking about investing the profit in other ventures that would not run the risk of being nationalized. Situations like that have arisen at various times and places, making diversification a legitimate option for owners and managements.

None of the three situations described above necessarily exclude the possibility of trying to achieve some kind of synergy with the existing business, which should always be the preferred alternative.

There is also a fourth reason why unrelated diversification may take place. There are examples of entrepreneurially minded businessmen who have simply become bored with managing businesses that were difficult to develop any further, and therefore started new ventures just to get back closer to the wellsprings of businessmanship. This is of course an irrational motive, but it is a human one and not at all uncommon. I mention it because the phenomenon does exist, and it is well to be aware of it.

Summary

The common characteristic of the situations described in this chapter is the creative element, the urge to remodel a business operation or start a new one. In the present decade, shop-minding-oriented managements have successively been succeeded and replaced by development-oriented managements. At the same time the business community has been forced to accept a growing degree of originality and personality in the new-style executives, and this has made the world of business a more stimulating and exciting place.

6 Some typical strategic situations

The purpose of this chapter is to give some general guidance in connection with situations that often arise in companies. The reason why I have included this chapter is that I, like other consultants, often run across concrete problems relating to the kind of situations described here. Most of these typical situations actually represent means for putting a strategy into practice, though as I have already pointed out there are no absolute definitions of what are means and what are ends in the hierarchy of strategy.

One example is that of companies which for various reasons both want and need to diversify their operations. The concept of diversification is so unpopular nowadays, as a result of the misplaced faith in universal management skills that was so widespread in the 1960s and 1970s, that the very word is off-putting to many people in top executive positions. I have therefore included a brief account of the background to the idea of diversification – without making any claim to give all the details or present any new research findings.

Another example is vertical integration, where in my business as a consultant I have often encountered the belief that it is possible to influence market shares and margins in a steady-state situation by taking over the next or previous stage of whatever chain of operations one is involved in.

Most of these typical situations have been dealt with at length by authors such as Michael Porter, Igor Ansoff, Kathryn R. Harrigan and Bruce Henderson.

Capacity expansion

Establishment of new companies is a prerequisite for the very existence of business – and so is capacity expansion. Yet most establishments and expansions would never have happened if it had been possible to foresee the actual medium-term outfall of the return on investment projections. If Messrs Assar Gabrielsson and Gustav Larsson had known back in 1927 that Volvo would take five years to break even, that company would probably never have been established. Similarly, capacity is often expanded in a way that does not show a profit in the short or medium term.

Schools of economics in the Western world have been massively criticized for the kind of ROI calculations they teach. The criticism focuses partly on the lack of strategic vision in investment decisions, pointing out that such decisions are taken primarily according to criteria of yield and not of strategy. As a result, companies often decide against investments that cannot be justified by present-value or payback calculations, but would nevertheless be sound and businesslike if viewed in a longer time frame than is normally adopted.

Capacity expansion is associated either with investment in plant or with investment in people. The first principal rule in connection with capacity expansion and investment is:

> The need for market orientation is greatest when the decision to invest is made because the structure of investment, whether in machinery or other facilities, must be taken up by production once the investment is made.

If an airline decides to invest in sixty DC-9s, those aircraft and no others must be filled with passengers. If a carmaker builds a factory to assemble a particular model, its capacity must be utilized to produce that model. These are truisms, yet they are not always remembered; decisions to expand capacity are not always made in the market-oriented perspective in which they ought to be made.

A second principal rule that has been amply borne out by empirical experience is:

> Generally speaking, in all companies and all industries, there is a correlation between rising weight of investment and falling profitability.

There are several reasons for this correlation. If a company has heavy capital costs committed to a facility, it tends to utilize that facility right down to the variable marginal cost in order to cover all its variable costs and some small contribution towards capital costs. There is therefore a strong tendency to trim prices, and with them margins, thereby reducing the return on investment. After all, the whole idea of investment is that capital costs are supposed to replace labour costs. This trade-off does not normally work well.

134

A third rule refers to more people-intensive and know-how-intensive industries and companies, which now account for a growing proportion of industry throughout the Western world:

> It is wrong to assign a low value to know-how-intensive companies just because of the low value of material assets on their balance sheets.

Analysts everywhere in the West have a tendency to underestimate the value of know-how-intensive companies in relation to their earnings on account of the smaller material assets that such companies always have in comparison with goods-producing companies. They put a higher value on a shipyard with capital assets worth a quarter of a billion dollars than on a successful service company that is earning high profits but has much less capital tied up in its operations. One of the advantages of people is that they are adaptable and can be taught new skills. If you own a shipyard or a processing plant your room for manoeuvre is limited, whereas if you head an organization of individuals you have a flexibility that greatly reduces your business risks.

Although service and know-how companies all over the world have consistently shown better profit records than manufacturing companies with a heavy investment structure, the analysts still persist in putting a low value on people-intensive companies when they ought to be doing the precise opposite.

In connection with capacity expansion there are in fact only two possible reasons for assuming that the extra capacity can be utilized:

1. the market is growing;
2. market shares can be taken.

Many decisions to expand capacity are founded more on wishful thinking than on realistic assessment. If the market is growing, the first question must obviously be whether the competition is doing anything about the capacity situation. A situation that is profitable for all concerned can easily deteriorate into the predicament in which a major ferry line on an expanding market found itself. That market was a 'duopoly', and both shipping companies simultaneously decided to order two giant ferries apiece to carry the growing traffic.

As to the second possibility, capturing market shares, this is generally harder than people imagine. Competing companies are usually run by ambitious people who will not willingly let go of their market shares. There are exceptions, however. There was an airline that let its competitors take large chunks of its market over a period of several years starting around 1980, because keeping them would have involved heavy losses; increased capacity had not been matched by increased demand.

A company in the chemical industry invested in a factory to produce a special alloying metal. It turned out that the new factory was capable of supplying 125% of the European market's total requirement. As a result, prices went through the floor and the conditions on which the investment calculation had been based suddenly changed.

My fourth principal rule runs as follows:

> Always try to rent capacity if by doing so you can test a decision to expand capacity before actually committing yourself to the investment.

To expand capacity by renting it always *looks* more expensive, because your variable costs rise sharply. It does however give you a chance to test the least certain veriables in your investment calculation, namely demand and price.

And now for the fifth and final rule:

> If you can, always let demand increase faster than capacity.

In the heyday of trend extrapolation before about 1975, capacity expansion was based on forecasts. In 1975 we found out just how unreliable forecasts were. But that kind of unbridled optimism is still around: the European car industry currently has an overcapacity of around two million standard-range cars a year. It is hard to believe that this can still be happening in 1987 after the sharp lesson of twelve years ago.

Establishment

The concept of establishment is strongly allied to that of capacity expansion. The latter, however, aims at being able

136

to deliver more of the same product to much the same market and much the same customers, whereas the former involves either a new product, new customers or a new market. A decision to establish is therefore fraught with more risk because it introduces a further unknown variable.

Establishment aimed at supplying a new product to existing customers and markets is also called organic diversification; the idea is to satisfy a broader part of the customers' spectrum of needs by widening the range of goods and services supplied. An example of this is Volvo's acquisition of Daf's car manufacturing operation in 1973. Family-size Volvos and subcompact Dafs are not of course bought by the same customers; the synergy in this case lay primarily in a strategic need to be able to offer dealers a wider range of cars that could be identified with Volvo. This made Volvo dealerships more attractive. The coverage and competence of the dealer organization is a key strategic factor in the passenger car business.

Another example can be taken from the world of finance. The establishment of stockbroking, leasing and finance companies by banks provides a good illustration of the kind of establishment known as organic diversification. A point to bear in mind in this context is:

> If you broaden your product, you may sometimes run into a very different trade logic. This makes it more essential than ever to understand the logic of business within the specific area of need concerned.

There are plenty of examples of companies who decided to take what seemed the very simple step of going into a related product area without realizing the differences in business conditions and trade logic. Rank Xerox's venture into computers is one of those examples. A lot of banks have tried unsuccessfully to compete in stockbroking. Advertising agencies and other consultancy firms with good track records in their own fields have tried to branch out into apparently related fields and done badly there.

Another main area of establishment is in new geographical markets. The globalization of industry offers numerous examples of the opportunities and risks connected with this kind of establishment. Atlas Copco, the Swedish compressed-air engineering company, owed a large part of its success to its establishment of sales companies in 49 countries. However, the return on this organization has not been so good because its rate of capital turnover and its productivity are low.

The globalization of the telecommunications industry is another interesting contemporary example. Establishment here is very expensive owing to differences in engineering systems. ITT gave up on its own US domestic market after investing about a billion dollars. It then tried to establish itself on a broad front on the European market, but was once more forced to give up due to technical and commercial difficulties, after which it merged with CGE of France.

In the meantime, Ericsson of Sweden is investing enormous sums trying to establish a foothold in the American market. It is very doubtful whether its investment calculations show any profit this side of the mid-1990s. But in 1986 Ericsson won three trial orders from American telephone companies, which was an important step forward.

Geographical establishment is often a matter of sheer survival. This is especially true in globalizing industries where the size of viable production runs makes it necessary to have a worldwide market.

The need for businessmanship is fundamental in an establishment context. The risks, as I have said, are greater than in the case of capacity expansion because they contain an extra unknown variable and are therefore that much harder to calculate. Knowledge of trade logic, financial staying power and competent businessmanship are essential ingredients in any successful establishment venture.

Diversification

The history of diversification is short but colourful. From being 'top of the pops' in business in the 1960s and early 1970s, diversification is now under a cloud. The pendulum has swung to concentration on main business. This, of course, can be attributed to globalization and other expressions of the economies of scale that have come to characterize so many industries today.

However, diversification has recently started to make a comeback, although now in a more balanced fashion and

138

with different motives. Many companies today are generating so much surplus capital through their main business, and at the same time finding their opportunities for expanding that main business so limited, that diversification looks like a good way of both investing their capital and spreading their risks.

Getting back to the history of diversification, we can trace the roots of its popularity in the 1960s to the then prevalent technocratic belief in a kind of management skill that was universally applicable to any kind of industry. This belief led in turn to the assumption and conviction that knowledge of the specific industry was a non-essential component of corporate management. All-round management competence was considered both necessary and sufficient for the running of any business.

It is remarkable to see how ITT under the legendary Harold Geenen became the very epitome of the diversified conglomerate. It is even more remarkable in that ITT today, some 15 years after Geenen's depature, is once more in the news by virtue of its retirement from its original principal business of telecommunications.

The present Chief Executive of ITT, Mr Araskog, took over an organization that covered everything from perfume to digital telephone exchanges and faced the task of generating a satisfactory capital yield from this vast conglomerate. As so often happens, its technocratic management had not encouraged entrepreneurial businessmanship, with the result that nearly all its heads of subsidiaries were cast in the same technocratic mould as the corporate top management. In the harsher competitive climate that came with the world energy crisis and the overvalued dollar, there arose a need for competitive management capability that was largely lacking in the ITT hierarchy. Araskog concentrated heavily on the telecommunications industry as the nucleus around which ITT was to construct its profitable base. After spending nearly a billion dollars trying to adapt System 12 to American standards, ITT gave up in 1986 and merged with CGE, which had its own reasons for looking for a global partner.

Thus after first having pursued an extreme policy of diversification and inspired many others to follow suit, ITT tried to reconcentrate into its original field of telecommunications and failed. It will be interesting to see what happens to ITT in the future.

It can be both interesting and instructive to ponder on the

disrepute into which diversification has fallen. If we study how diversified conglomerates got to be that way – and there are examples available for study in every country – we nearly always find an extremely entrepeneurial owner or chief executive who with unfailing business instinct built up a diversified empire.

Later we can usually trace a gradual decline of profitability starting with the rise to power of a technocratically inclined top management that lacks knowledge of the trade logic of the industries into which the conglomerate has expanded. These new managements often have a strong financial bias and run their groups mainly according to the criteria of finance rather than those of business strategy.

At this stage the view usually becomes prevalent that there is a need to concentrate – which indeed there is. A process of contraction then sets in, marked by concentration on certain areas and a reduction in the size of the conglomerate.

Some of the reasons for these phenomena of falling profitability and contraction can, I think, be sought in factors that gradually come to dominate the corporate culture of the conglomerate's subsidiaries. The technocratic corporate management tends to appoint people of its own ilk to head the subsidiaries. The results are often disappointing because those people lack a feeling for business and knowledge of the trade logic of the industries concerned.

As I see it, the conclusion to be drawn from the pattern I have described provides one of the prime rules of diversification:

> The scope of a diversified operation is limited by the business ability of the group management to appoint the right people as heads of subsidiaries and to act as a sparring partner for the individual companies in matters of business strategy.

Diversification is now on the way back, albeit for different reasons than before. In the first place managements in some countries are much more business oriented nowadays, and have both the competence and the courage to diversify. In the second place there are companies with strong positive cash flows looking for ways to spread their risks and invest their money profitably. Awareness of the importance of trade logic to success in business is helping to avoid the traps which previously caused diversification to fall into disfavour

Let us close this section on diversification by reviewing the motives for it. The possible motives are:

1. *Risk spreading*, i.e. financial equalization over a period of time.
2. *Financial motives*; the ROI is judged to be better than alternative investment opportunities.
3. *Synergies* with existing lines of business are judged to be sufficiently favourable to the whole to justify diversification.
4. *Entrepreneurial motives*; the risk involved in diversifying is seen as a challenge.

Deregulation

Deregulation in a strategic context refers to industries or areas of supply in which competition was formerly strongly restricted and where the restrictions have now been eased or abolished. The classic case that springs to most people's minds is the Carter Administration's deregulation of domestic passenger air traffic in the United States, which started in 1978.

Deregulation of telecommunications in the United States, of banking and currency trading in Western Europe, etc., has followed in quick succession and created a new type of strategic situation that hardly existed before 1978.

To understand deregulation and the business opportunities it will offer, we must first try to understand the factors the originally led to regulation and how the situation in the world has changed since then. In the case of civil aviation it was the issue of safety that prompted governments all over the world after the end of the Second World War to decide that regulation was necessary. The underlying view was that unrestricted competition would tempt airlines to cut corners on safety.

The record shows in fact that air safety has improved steadily and has now reached a level that was once almost unimamginable. With the exception of 1985, the number of deaths in air traffic accidents – per passenger mile or by any other yardstick – has steadily declined since the beginning of the 1960s.

Deregulation thus needs to be analysed on the basis of the factors that led to regulation in the first place.

The disadvantages of regulation have grown more apparent in the light of the widespread growth in efficiency of private enterprise that has taken place as a result of such stimuli as the energy crisis in the mid-1970s. It has become increasingly plain that regulated industries are decidedly inferior to free ones in terms of productivity. This is of course a result of the 'deadwood' that organizations inevitably accumulate when shielded from competition. As governments have found it progressively harder to balance their budgets, the inefficiency of regulated industries has become more of a thorn in their flesh. This is probably one of the reasons for the tide of deregulation that is now sweeping the Western world.

The first point to consider in connection with deregulation is this:

> Think through the factors that originally gave rise to regulation of the industry, and how those factors have changed.

You must go to a fairly high level of abstraction to find similarities between deregulated industries. There is a high degree of heterogeneity in industry-specific factors, but nevertheless there are some general conclusions to be drawn. Perhaps the most important observation is this:

> In a deregulated industry, ability to compete and will to compete are badly atrophied in comparison with outside industry.

Herein, of course, lies the threat that faces companies in the industry when it is deregulated. Regulated industries tend to get populated by executives of a decidedly more bureaucratic turn of mind than in industries exposed to competition. This will naturally be reflected in corporate culture with regard to risk taking, enterprise, customers, etc. Come deregulation, those companies are thrown bodily into the cold water of competition, which in most cases is a profound culture shock. So be alert for cultural changes in connection with deregulation.

If we switch to the other side of the fence and observe the business opportunties that come with deregulation, this is a good rule to follow:

> Consider carefully all the unsatisfied needs which exist in the regulated area and which can now be satisfied.

142

Companies in a regulated industry have not always neglected to satisfy needs because they were incapable of competing; the situation may be that companies in that industry have been *forbidden* to compete in certain areas. Swedish bank, for example, were not allowed to offer certain kinds of loans with certain kinds of risks – an opportunity that was open to other finance institutes on the market. In such cases deregulation makes companies in the industry more competitive, not less so.

If you once more put yourself in the place of the regulated industry, I would recommend a vigorous strategic effort based on the new opportunties that will arise:

> The regulated industry should try to be *proactive* to new business opportunities, thereby winning competitive advantages over other companies in the industry and over new competitors.

By 'proactive' I mean anticipating changes before they happen instead of reacting to them afterwards – a sure way to get left behind.

Another common characteristic of deregulation is the strong boost it always gives to logic and business dynamics. The trade logic of the industry may change in fundamental respects, generating new threats and new opportunities. The dynamics of the business are bound to be affected in that creativity appears on the scene and makes itself much more keenly felt than before. Unbridled and unthinking dynamism can of course lead to disaster. It did so in the case of the airline Branif, who immediately after deregulation opened 27 new air routes and subsequently went bankrupt.

The world-wide move to deregulate telecommunications initiated the restructuring and globalization of the industry that I have cited by way of example several times in this book.

Vertical integration

Like diversification, vertical integration was at one time something of a management fad, though that was several decades ago. A classic example is the Singer sewing-machine company, which in its day integrated the whole production chain from lumber and iron ore to finished sewing machines.

The great majority of industries have undergone a realignment towards less integration. They are making fewer and fewer parts of the finished product, and buying more and more. An interesting exception, in some respects, is the automobile industry. Back in the 1910s and 1920s there were a host of manufacturers of automobile components – even of whole chassis. This enabled the carmaker to pick various components out of printed catalogues and put his own stamp on the finished product in the form of body and radiator grille styling.

General Motors, one of the world's largest producers of passenger cars, today faces difficulties. It is interesting to note that General Motors has the highest degree of vertical integration among car producers in the Western hemisphere. The degree of vertical integration exceeds 60%, compared with Ford, about 45%; Chrysler, about 37%; and Toyota, less than 25%. One can easily draw the conclusion that market transactions are more efficient than the internal transactions which are characteristic of vertical integration.

The main trend, however, is clear. More and more industries are cutting down on integration and buying more. There are a couple of interesting but sometimes overlooked effects of this trend.

The first one is that the relative importance of the purchasing function in companies is increasing. Yet purchasing is often treated as a poor relation; it is by no means always represented at top management level, or made the subject of a carefully considered departmental strategy.

The second effect of diminishing vertical integration is the need to speed up capital turnover in order to sustain the level of return on investment. When the in-house value-added component of the product grows smaller, then obviously the turnover of working capital must grow correspondingly greater to yield the same ROI. More interest is being taken nowadays in in-house added value relative to the size of the workforce and relative to capital, so this is a point that bears watching.

> Vertical integration means that market transactions are replaced by internal transactions.

To principle, all functions of a business operation can be organized as separate companies. You can hive off a computer section, a manufacturing facility, a sales organization or

144

other parts of the administrative apparatus. A decision on vertical integration, then, is essentially a decision whether to 'manufacture' products and services yourself or buy them from outside sources. Vertical integration decisions are therefore akin to establishment decisions, and are based on whether it is judged more profitable to make or buy. Naturally, however, the decision is not just a matter of profitability but very much one of strategy.

> A decision on verticial integration can be based either on cost-saving criteria or on strategic considerations.

One alternative, then, is to have an internal unit whose capacity is utilized exclusively by your own company. The goals for that unit are set according to various cost-effectiveness criteria and its operations, whether they relate to goods or services, are regarded as a functional part of the whole with no separate corporate mission.

The other alternative is to treat the function concerned as a business unit. It is assigned its own corporate mission on the usual basis of needs, product, customer and competitors. This approach naturally assumes that the unit will also deliver to other customers outside your own organization.

> The next link in the integration chain usually is governed by an entirely different kind of trade logic.

To cite the example of Singer once more, the trade logic of the lumber industry that delivers the base of the sewing machine is obviously quite different from that of the sewing-machine industry itself. In other cases, however, the distinction is not so clear. In the transport sector, one might easily suppose that the forwarding agency business shares a common trade logic with air cargo or trucking. But in fact it does not. The true structure in this particular example is very hard to discern because forwarding agents traditionally wear more hats, including those of freight wholesalers and suppliers of transportation.

The advantages of vertical integration can be listed as follows:

1. You have a coordinated business, which makes it much easier to monitor, control and audit your operations.
2. You have much better access to market information about the area in question. Vertical integration means that you are actually in another line of business, with whatever advantages accrue from that fact.

145

3. Integration gives you a high degree of stability in your relations. The links in a portfolio encourage continuous communication and business.
4. In addition to knowledge of trade logic, vertical integration provides knowledge of the technology of the industry concerned (which is a subset of trade logic).
5. In many cases vertical integration also gives you better opportunties for differentiating your own product. A foothold in another industry increases your ability to vary your product.

All these advantages of vertical integration are of a kind that is less highly appreciated than market transactions according to the current world-wide trend towards liberalization. Control and auditing, for example, are no longer regarded as optimum ways of making operations more efficient. The disadvantages listed below are therefore more apparent now than they used to be.

1. Vertical integration bypasses market forces and is therefore apt to generate deadwood in the organization.
2. It opens the door to a policy of subsidiaries that distorts the competition picture and thereby obscures the issues of viability.
3. It gives you a false position of negotiating strength that does not match the reality of free negotiations on the open market.
4. It gives you a false sense of security by creating an artificial captive market.
5. This false sense of security erodes your will and ability to compete.

Vertical integration has had its champions, especially in socialist economies. They have a weakness for big combines with far-reaching vertical integration as the answer to all kinds of problems like employment and investment. The reason for this may be the didactic clarity that a high degree of vertical integration always displays. If you can point to an iron mine and trace its products through a chain of other operations culminating in cars or refrigerators, the relationships in the structure of industry are clear and easy to communicate.

Behind many cases of vertical integration we find a large measure of self-deception or misconception – and this is still true today. The commonest fallacy is the belief that you can eliminate competition at a given stage by dominating that stage. Here follows a list of some of the prevalent illusions concerning vertical integration:

1. A strong position on the market at one stage can be carried over to another stage — In the consumer cooperative movement and other conglomerates this fallacy has often been responsible for investment decisions which later led to all the disadvantages listed above.
2. Internal trading makes it possible to dispense with a sales force and simplify administration, thereby saving overhead costs — This of course is a typical tenet of planning economy whch reflects a touching faith in central control as an alternative to control by market forces.
3. By buying up the link immediately before or after us in the production and distribution chain we can shore up a strategically weak business — This may be true in some exceptional cases, but not very often. The logic of each industry must be judged on its own merits, and that is also true in this case unless it is a matter of diversifying to spread risks.
4. Knowledge of an industry can be utilized in the industry before or after it in the chain in order to give a competitive edge — This may be possible, but if so the supposed advantages must be carefully scrutinized to check that there are no fallacies hidden in the logic.

There are plenty of examples of how entrepreneurship has produced spectacular improvements in profitability by breaking the chains of vertical integration. This is probably the chief explanation of the fact that business as a whole is now moving towards a lower degree of integration. Car manufacturers who own their own export shipping lines pay no less for transportation than those who use regular ro-ro carriers. Car manufacturers who make their own transmissions get them no cheaper than those who buy from specialist gearbox manufacturers. The list could be extended.

I think that one of the reasons why vertical integration achieved such wide popularity during the technocratic era was that the calculable economies of scale were so readily apparent, whereas the economies of *small* scale, such as entrepreneurship and competitive ability, were not amenable to quantitative analysis.

Acquisition

The hierarchy of strategy sometimes makes the terminology ambiguous. Acquisition's, mergers and disinvestments are, to my mind, more operational means of implementing strategies in practice than principal strategic alternatives in themselves. In this section we shall confine ourselves to acquisition, disinvestment being simply the mirror image of the same thing.

We can distinguish three rational motives for acquisition:

1. to fill a gap in a portfolio;
2. to invest a surplus;
3. to strengthen a business unit.

To these three we must add a fourth which is irrational in terms of business but nonetheless extremely common, namely the empire-building urge.

This irrational motive is so common, albeit mostly concealed and explained away by other ostensible motives, that I felt I had to mention it, though I am not going to subject it here to a detailed examination in terms of behavioral science. However, it is an excellent thing if a management has the honesty to acknowledge, at least to itself, that its prime reason for acquisition is to extend its power.

When I speak of filling a gap in a portfolio I am of course referring to synergistic portfolios with some small kind of shared resource. The aim may be to acquire a missing product to satisfy the structure of customer needs in a given area, to utilize the capacity of an underemployed distribution channel or production facility, or something else. Volvo's acquisition of Daf was originally prompted by the need to strengthen its bargaining position with dealers by adding a smaller and cheaper car to its range. A data consultancy firm that buys up a firm of training specialists obviously plans to satisfy its customer's need for training in conjunction with the installation and operation of computer systems.

Investing a surplus is often the underlying motive in boom periods when companies' cash flows take an upturn. Although there are nearly always opportunities for investing in the investor's own principal business, considerations of risk or timing may make it advisable to put the money into something else.

Closely akin to the cash-investment motive is that of acquiring a badly managed company. Somebody may have had the opportunity to observe at close range how a mangement has handled its business, and come to the conclusion that he could quickly improve the result of that business by buying it and putting in new management. Such a situation naturally represents a business opportunity where the investment in acquisition can pay a handsome dividend.

The third rational motive for acquisiton is to strengthen a business unit. The item acquired may be a competitor, a supplier, a new distribution channel or a new technology. Buying out a competitor to get a bigger market share may be justified in situations where there are tangible economies of scale to be won in manufacturing or distribution. In the express package business in the United States, for example, market share is crucial to the fequency of delivery in a given district and thus to a company's ability to make express deliveries at a reasonable cost. In other cases there are substantial economies to be made through longer production runs. However, the advance of modern production technology has made this last case less typical now than it used to be. Economies of scale in production are often overrated as a competitive advantage.

Regardless of its motive for acquisition, the acquiring company must assess the value of the potential acquiree as a basis for negotiations. Empirical data show that in 80% of all acquisitions the buyer, two years after the event, considers the acquistion a disappointment, while about the same proportion of sellers are satisfied with the deal they made. In other words, acquisition is a very difficult art as regards both strategic assessment and operative handling.

> The mistake most often made by acquirers is to misjudge the strategic position and operational skill of the aquiree.

It sometimes happens that companies stop allocating resources to any forward-looking purpose. They drop all R&D, cut back their sales force to a minimum, make no new investments in production plant, and so on. By doing so they create what is known as a 'soufflé company', which means a company with a slimmed-down balance sheet and a grossly inflated bottom line. The object of the exercise is of course to be able to show a potential buyer evidence of an amazing growth in profits and a high return on investment – evidence on which the selling price will be based.

One of the most important things the buyer must do, then, is to judge the strategic attractiveness of the potential aquiree balanced against the latter's operational ability. The table in Fig. 27 shows how two businesses with the same ROI can differ very widely in their future profit potential.

Fig. 27 Expectations of profitability

Assessment	Company A	Company B
Return on investment	20%	20%
Market share	small	large
Relative market share	small	large
Relative product quality	low	high
Capital-to-turnover ratio	high	low
Capital per employee	low	high
Added value per employee	average	average
Market growth	low	high
Outlook	excellent	disastrous

The fact that companies A and B in Fig. 27 show the same return on investment may be simply a coincidence, or it may be attributable to a marked difference in management competence between the companies. As in all other business situations, it is necessary to grasp the trade logic under which the aquiree operates in order to make a correct assessment of its present performance.

There is a wealth of literature on the subject, describing checklists, screening methods and other techniques applicable to acquistion. In this context I have made a selection of questions that are of crucial importance to any company contemplating an acquisition:

1. How much profit do we expect the acquiree to generate? It is becoming increasingly common practice to link the purchase price to the growth rate of the acquiree's earnings, so that the seller is made to give a distinct undertaking. Expectations of future earnings must of course be weighed against the purchase price, so an assessment of how realistic those expectations are is often a useful check question.
2. Can any weakness in the acquiree be corrected? Replacing the management is one possibility already mentioned. In other cases the buyer may have noted weaknesses in marketing organization, production or other functions that he can immediately put right and thereby create the necessary conditions for a speedy improvement in profitability.

3. Will the acquisition complement the present portfolio, and if so how?

   Advocates of planned acquisitions often cite as motives synergies which do not in fact exist. Especially in cases where the real motive is empire-building, there is a tendency to camouflage that motive by pointing to synergies of a diffuse nature. It is of course perfectly legitimate to make such bogus synergies the cover story for public consumption, as long as you are honest enough with yourself to recognize your true motives.

4. How much is the acquisition worth?

   The implication of this question is that you proceed from the top price you are willing to pay in view of the value that the aquisition can have for your own company. This kind of reasoning is often very helpful in defining the framework for negotiations. Though due deliberation before decision is a virtue as far as acquisitions are concerned, the time factor may be a decisive constraint.

The purpose of this section has been to clarify the true motives for acquisition and to offer a few points to ponder and check questions to ask. Leaving the structural aspects of acquisition, I would like to mention in conclusion that I have known heads of companies who have made entrepreneurial acquisitions, with no structural base and with very little formal analysis, that turned out to be enormously successful. In one particular instance, a medium-sized acquisition deal was concluded in two days, much to the annoyance of two other companies that had been negotiating with the seller for a couple of months. Knowledge of the 'technology' of acquisition is essential and can save a lot of time.

Declining industries

There is now plenty of good theoretical literature on declining industries. One example is Kathryn R. Harrigan's thesis 'Strategies for declining industries'.

My main message with regard to stagnating industries is twofold:

1. Creative businessmanship is a commodity in short supply.
2. Traditional strategy theories do more harm than good.

The prevailing theory in situations of decline is to regard business units in the afflicted industries as 'dogs'. According to received theory, a good company should not own such business units but should sell them. This of course raises the question of where to find a gullible buyer willing to pay for the privilege of taking over a business that is going to lose him a packet of money. For a long time, many European governments found themselves in the position of feeling obliged to take over companies in stagnant and declining industries. The will to compete was at a low ebb in the mid-1970s, with the result that industries in trouble were too easily given up as hopeless cases.

A number of theoretical portfolio models, of which the BCG matrix is the best known, use strategic attractiveness as a basis for classifying business units, with heavy emphasis on growth trends and profitability in the industry. Such a classification does of course have some values, e.g. in connection with assessment of what capital and management resources need to be injected. But a destructive element enters the picture when business units in declining industries, often on flimsy grounds, are consigned to a list of companies to be 'milked' or 'harvested'.

The idea, according to strategic portfolio theory, is to try to squeeze out the capital invested in the business unit. Sometimes, undoubtedly, this is the right thing to do. But the great objection to this procedure is that it is entirely introspective and ignores what is going on in the outside world. What it amounts to is resigning from the market and foregoing the chance to apply creative business strategies. This attitude manifests itself in the milking of cash flows and the strangulation of investment in development, production technology and marketing. In actual practice the dividing line between 'milking' and pulling out of the industry is very fine.

Another consequence of these traditional methods of classification is the alarm and despondency they generate. Morale in the business unit plunges, and the creative drain accelerates.

Research by Hamersh and Silk and others has shown that such business units in declining industries will, given a competent management that works out its strategies with care and applies them with vigour, be much more profitable than others where the people have a strong suspicion that they are candidates for disinvestment or milking.

Another important finding of this research is that success

in declining industries is closely associated with strategic leadership ability in the sense of being able to identify, create and exploit growth segments within the declining industry. Emphasis on customer-perceived product quality, systematic and consistent improvement of production efficiency and capital deployment are other major hallmarks of successful companies in declining industries.

It seems on the face of it that the choice of growth segments in declining industries implies avoidance of competition in such industries. In fact one of the most vital of strategic skills is that of being in the right industry and the right segment, and consequently spending a lot of time and resources on analysis of the industry in an effort to detect the growth segments that are always there somewhere.

The ability to identify growth segments is closely associated with my other main point, i.e. the shortage of strategic management ability in declining industries. It lies in the nature of the entrepreneur to gravitate away from difficult, low-growth environments towards more dynamic and expansive environments. So naturally, individuals with strategic management ability tend to move out of decclining industries into growing industries. This is one of the major problems of declining industries, and at the same time a major opportunity. One large American corporation has made it a qualification for executive recruitment to have headed a business unit in a declining industry. Managers with the experience behind them have highly developed competitive skills that deserve due recognition.

With the departure of creative and entrepreneurially minded individuals, declining industries generally come to be dominated by individuals with a more technocratic bias. This exacerbates the problems of those industries.

Growth industries

Companies in extreme growth industries have a tendency to totally neglect the need for strategic management. Comments like 'Strategy? What's that? Business is about making money are typically heard in situations where running a business at a profit looks easy.

Growth industries are characterized by having a growth rate a few percentage points higher than the growth of GNP.

They are further characterized, almost invariably, by having a new product that satisfies new demands which, however, can be traced back to old needs. Often the new product has superseded an older one, as cars superseded horses and buggies – usually with the result that some other industry has slowly or abruptly gone into decline. In other cases, like personal computers and mobile telephones, the new product does not replace an older one but helps to make individuals and companies more productive.

In both these cases we see the rise of a new industry, which always develops its own trade logic.

The situation in fast-growing industries is always that demand outstrips supply. This means, of course, that products can nearly always be sold. And that in turn means that customer-perceived quality is a much less important consideration than in normal industries.

Excess demand and lack of sales resistance often give rise to an unqualified optimism that approaches the nature of hubris. Everything seems easy, and the business just rolls in. Because so few demands are made on companies in the industry, managements are often inept or downright incompetent.

> The personal computer dealership business is an outstanding example. At one time the sky was the limit – until the time came when the 'novelty demand' was satisfied and sales resistance began to rear its ugly head. This revealed just how little business ability many of the actors on the scene possessed. Readiness to face the hard and exacting process of actually managing a business was totally lacking in many cases.

In this kind of situation, strategic management tends to be regarded in the nature of an academic luxury, and there is a temptation to look down on the management skills that others have been forced to acquire.

Time and time again we find examples of how companies that have learned strategic management skills during periods of extreme growth have been the ones that have eventually taken the lead in developing and restructuring their industries, even if they were not the ones who grabbed the biggest market shares at the height of the growth phase.

Here, then, is a ground rule:

A businesslike company in an extreme growth industry can, by preparing for normal growth conditions, emerge from the inevitable normalization to come as one of the leaders of its industry.

Relatively little attention is paid to customer-perceived quality by fast-growing industries. The excess demand situation creates a 'seller's market'. The change which so many companies in such industries have failed to anticipate is the transition from a seller's to a buyer's market and the tougher demands they face as a result. The reorientation of the industry is not made any easier by the fact that the change usually comes about much more abruptly than anyone imagined it would. The situation in the data consultancy business shifted from excess demand to excess supply within a couple of months. There are many examples of such sudden changes and the drastic effects they have had on companies in the industries concerned.

> Try to improve customer-perceived quality instead of trying to hang on to your market share.

Experience shows that the companies who concentrate most on growth and on holding or expanding their market shares in a fast-growing industry are the ones who are hardest hit by the transition to normal growth or stagnation. So if you want to survive as a separate company and maybe even take the lead in developing the structure of your industry, you should pay more attention to customer-perceived quality than to market share. The two are not necessarily mutually exclusive, but it is crucial to your corporate culture which of them you focus on.

To sum up, then, here are the rules for achieving strategic leadership in a fast-growing industry:

> 1. Build up management skills and go for strategic competence while the growth phase is still in progress.
> 2. Focus on customer-perceived qualtiy instead of trying to hang on to market share.
> 3. Do not get stuck in the growth phase by dimensioning your resources according to an extrapolated growth curve.
> 4. Try to assess the future structure of the industry, e.g. by drawing parallels with other industries that have previously passed through similar phases.

Many fast-growing companies have confirmed the truth of the old saying that 'pride goeth before a fall', whether their growth was due to general expansion of the industry or a temporarily very strong competitive position.

7 Key questions in strategy development processes

Strategic management resources

Not all the people in executive positions in companies have seen enough strategy processes to give them experience to abstract from and apply in a real-life strategic situation. Training in strategic management is rare and is only sporadically available, one reason for which is that the subject lacks a received methodology. The big international management schools do give such training to a certain extent, but it is preferable to put the entire top management of a company through a course of strategic management training together, with their own company as a case to practise on. One way is to organize strategic development seminars on a pattern that largely follows the chapter headings in this book, i.e. strategic management, the structure of strategy, the process of strategy and strategies for business development – or some other scheme more relevant to the individual company.

It is also becoming increasingly necessary to try and identify individuals with an aptitude for strategic business management. Operative skills and wholehearted commitment to leadership are not always accompanied by the talents needed to be able to lead a company to a position of strength through business development.

The kindest thing to do in the short term is to let operatively inclined executives keep their jobs. This is not in the best long-term interests of either the individual or the company, but it is the easiest way out in the short term and is therefore often chosen. The optimum long-term policy for both individuals and companies is of course to encourage strategic leadership where it is needed.

There has been a great reluctance to accept the need for a fresh view of top management qualifications, but the trend is unmistakable and is becoming steadily clearer. Bad management is a bad thing for everybody concerned, and it is not in fact necessary to be ruthless to correct ill-advised promotions.

The former overemphasis on the analytical element in strategy has often had a deterrent effect on the ambitions of medium-sized companies to embark on strategy development processes.

Any self-respecting management consultant naturally claims to be able to handle a strategy development process. In the hierarchy of consultancy those who deal in abstract issues are considered a cut above the common herd, which impels many consultants to claim expertise on strategic processes. It is undoubtedly true that many consultants have been involved in strategic planning processes according to the planning technocracy model, but fewer have had occasion to take part in a complete process conducted according to the modern principles of business development. So check your consultants' qualifications and experience in strategy development with care: proclamation of a unilateral belief in any particular model or technique should be regarded as a warning signal, not a road to salvation.

I have found it hard to interest people in questions of strategy unless they related to some very large or well-known company, but in fact there is seldom any correlation between the nature of the strategic problem and the size of the company.

While on the subject of consultants, I would like to point out that different consultants can do most good at different stages of the process – analysis, strategy determintion and implementation. What is most needed at the analytical stage is a capacity for deductive thinking. Strategy determination requires that, too, but also creativity and strategic experience. The implementation stage, finally, calls for a high degree of process knowledge, i.e. knowledge of how to handle people.

Planning

Not only strategic planning in particular but planning in general are currently the target of a cannonade of criticism from business-minded people who have been deeply disappointed in the ability, or rather inability, of planning to

157

contribute to sound business development. There is therefore a strong tendency nowadays to 'throw out planning with the bathwater' and maintain that all planning is basically meaningless. The real situation is not that simple. Planning still has an essential part to play in a company: what was wrong was to let planning control strategy development instead of the other way around.

If the airline opts for a strategy that contradicts the received logic of its industry by proposing to run a frequent schedule of flights with small aircraft on intercontinental routes, this poses a planning problem which must be solved and which will have clear consequences in capital procurement, pilot training and other areas.

Planning should not be done in separate staff organizations, but integrated with operations. The reason is that if planning becomes the province of staff organizations, an intellectual elite of planning technocrats will arise from which, perish the thought, top executives with no actual business experience may eventually be recruited direct. Naturally the business organization must be in control of planning, not vice versa. In fact it would be a good idea to quarantine all staffs for about the next ten years to avoid the risk of overeducated academics seizing control from businessmen (the McNamara syndrome).

Strategies for what?

Imagine that you are President of the Finnish subsidiary of a major international automotive corporation, that your parent company has just decided to stop selling tractors in your territory, and that from your point of view there seems to be a lack of strategic thinking at Head Office. This is by no means an uncommon experience in business life. If you yourself are strategically minded but must constantly relate your area of responsibility to a greater whole which you perceive as being without strategy, then you have a problem.

The same thing applies if you are a department head or the head of a business unit in a corporation. If you have strategic ability, you may easily get the feeling that you are out of tune with corporate thinking. A situation like this calls for a large measure of diplomacy as you set out for your goal, which of course must be to get a clear strategic picture of the whole so that you can run your part of it accordingly.

If you have filled your quota of tractor sales only to have tractors pulled from under you off the Finnish market, this is obviously not your fault; it means there is a lack of strategic clarity at Head Office level that must be dealt with. There are plenty of sales company, business unit and department heads who have strategic ability themselves but feel they are working in a strategic vacuum. To all of them I can offer the comforting thought that things are getting better all the time. A switch from administrative to strategic top management can take place with remarkable speed, and when it happens it brings with it an increased respect for strategic thinking far down in the organization.

There is a phenomenon called strategic tunnel vision that company executives ought to be aware of. It affects competition-oriented company heads who have excellent track records but who are apt to lose the strategic overview in tight situations and start trying to optimize conditions that are wrong and ought to be changed; they try to do things right instead of doing the right things. There are plenty of examples of how managements try to cling to an outdated corporate mission or production apparatus and sacrifice profitable parts of their companies in an effort to shore up a fundamentally unprofitable and obsolete structure of production.

I have seen several examples in Sweden. One is the building industry, where most companies are trying to stay in the contracting business although it is almost impossible for them to do much better than break even. Another is the shipping industry, where companies tend to sell off stocks and real estate to commit more and more resources to a business that has little chance of showing a profit over a whole business cycle.

If you as an executive are responsible for an operation that in your opinion is following a steady strategic course it might be a good idea, as I have mentioned before, to run a strategic audit, i.e. a review of the clarity of your strategies. The technique involves examining the elements of strategy to determine whether the company's various functions are in fact operating in a manner consistent with its overall strategy. Just as a marketing audit can be a most efficacious alarm clock, so can a strategic audit be a real shot in the arm that will improve the company's health in several respects.

Structural problems of strategy

A problem of the structure of strategy that has not been dealt with in the preceding chapters, but which is important in a strategic context, is the time aspect. Neither natural science, political philosophy nor business strategy can be divorced from the times in which they exist. This means that company managements must locate their strategic thinking at the right point on the time axis to avoid having the process go sour due to bad timing. I can think of many examples of highly strategic investments in forestry and shipping that led to the bankruptcy courts because of quirks in the business cycle. Two key variables in the determination of strategic horizons are needs and their development on the one hand, and technology and its development on the other.

Another structural problem of strategy, this one concerning the structures of industries, is the case where companies in a given industry cut their own throats by overinvesting. One example is shipping companies engaged in ferry traffic on a particular route where one of the competing lines suddenly decides to order jumbo ferries for passenger and commerical vehicle transport. If there is little chance of wiping out the competition, the investment is made in some sort of expectation of being able to attract more passengers and more vehicle traffic at unchanged prices. This type of trend extrapolation is regrettably all too common and usually leads to losses for all concerned.

In one case, however, involving a hotel construction project by a certain company in a medium-sized city, a similar situation was countered by a competitor's announcement of such a gigantic planned increase in capacity that the two companies finally talked things over between them and were able to head off a threatening no-win situation.

In short: the capacity of an industry in relation to the size of the market it serves is an essential factor.

The inward life of a company

There are many pitfalls along the way in a strategy development process. One of them lies in trying to get exact answers to every question and striving for precision at the expense of

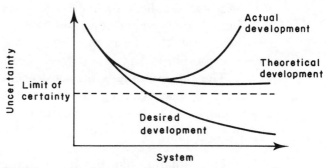

Fig. 28 Thornell's uncertainty relation. All planning activities are subject
to a degree of uncertainty which the planners want to minimize. They can
do that by using some kind of system in their planning, in the hope that
more advanced systems will lead to less uncertainty. There is however a
limit to this, set by totally unpredictable factors. When you reach that limit
you lose your grip on the whole and concentrate instead on analysing details
– WHICH ONLY INCREASES YOUR UNCERTAINTY.

If you do not measure the uncertainty you want to reduce, you will not
know how far to go in system development, with the consequence that in
most cases you will probably go too far and wind up with a case of
overadministration.

tempo. Experience has proved that if you worry too much
about details, the whole process can easily get bogged down.
My advice, then, is to take short-cuts if you have to, and be
constantly alert to the risk of getting unproductively hung up
on non-essentials.

There is a tendency, especially in companies with a fact-
finding or analytical culture, to constantly increase the
number of options instead of choosing between options. All
business involves risk. The risks should of course be mini-
mized, but can never be elminated. This self-evidence fact
may be deliberately suppressed in some cultures, which calls
for *well-founded simplifications*. 'Thornell's uncertainty
relation' is reproduced in Fig. 28 with the text in full; it
illustrates the need to move on from risk analysis to risk
taking in business.

Another phenomenon that is not uncommon is the desira-
bility of *overlapping structures*. By this I mean that many
industries need several forms of organization, especially on
the marketing side, which are not mutually exclusive but to
some extent sell the same goods and services.

An example is the freight agency business, in which the
sale of transporation is traditionally divided by means of
transport – road, rail, air, sea, etc. An outside consultant
notes that what the industry is actually doing is reducing the
amount of capital its customers need to have to keep tied up

161

in stocks. So the thing to do is not to sell means of transport but to analyse customers' capital turnover and offer advice on that basis as to the most suitable method of transportation.

The only trouble is that customers do not buy on that basis. Their puchasing structure still largely follows the old means-of-transport-based pattern, with the exception of a few avant-garde customers who have moved ahead of the rest of the market.

In a situation like this it is definitely advisable to have overlapping organizational structures, i.e. to have one organization selling in the traditional way, but also another organization to build up the new goods flow administration know-how and sell it as a product. This way your company gains competence while at the same time keeping pace with the evolution of the market. Markets do not in fact always act in their own theoretical best interests, and it behoves the seller to be patient and wait for the market to learn better.

Another example is a fast-expanding industry like data consultancy. New segments are constantly appearing, and in many cases the work done for the client is of the same kind, even though the starting points may differ. In this kind of environment, too, it can make sense to have overlapping structures, partly because customers' preferences vary and partly to allow development to be angled on the basis of organizational divisions. In the data consultancy industry it is possible to set up a data strategy unit whose area of operations will naturally overlap that of the existing unit responsible for administrative development.

Even in totally different contexts there may be good grounds for abandoning a strictly linear organization for the sake of encouraging development or dealing more efficiently with customers. It is more important to direct the maximum amount of energy towards the market than to maintain a linear organization just to satisfy demands from inside the organization.

Another key question that affects the inward life of a company is the often necessary replacement of a largely administrative management by a more development-minded or entrepreneurial one. Those who advocate the need for more businessmanship and discuss the pros and cons of entrepreneurship at seminars and on other occasions are generally applauded and can expect agreement that businessmen ought to be put back into key positions. But it has proved much harder to go from words to reality.

162

It seems to be much easier to accept businessmanship and entrepreneurial personalities in theory than in practice. Leading business-minded people is one of the high arts of business and, in my opinion, one of the richest sources of revival of the business spirit in companies.

Having developed a strategy – what next?

In some industries and in some development situations it may make sense to start thinking about the development of a strategy to *follow* the process you have just initiated or are currently involved in. It may sound somewhat exaggerated, but there are situations in which the next step after strategy development needs to be considered at an early stage.

Such a situation can arise in a service-producing company that has been through a highly efficient strategy development process. The employees have been given clear goals to aim at and a clear strategic course to follow, and this has substantially raised the energy level of the whole organization, stimulating quick-turnover business.

The danger here is that the stimulus provided by strategic clarity will gradually wear off and that exaggerated expectations will be built up which cannot be fulfilled. In this kind of situation it is a good idea to start thinking about finding ways to gradually add new values that will help to sustain high motivation and good business.

Another situation in which a need arose to think about 'strategies beyond the strategies' occurred in the airfreight business, where the supply grew explosively without relation to demand with the introduction of wide-bodied aircraft in the mid-1970s. The primary strategic need in a five-year perspective was to find ways of differentiating the product to assure survival in the medium term. However, it is clear that the structure of world trade is developing in a manner highly favourable to airfreight. So trimmings, product differentiation and cutbacks must be made against a background of a future offering rich opportunities for growth, and current strategy development must take this into account.

A third situation in which 'post-strategic' thinking is desirable is in a manufacturing industry that is forced to restructure itself as a result of runaway overcapacity. The process of restructuring will be complete within a normal strategic horizon of, say, three to six years.

A company in that industry needs to have a business development strategy ready for use after restructuring, if it does not want to go on scaling down its operations and waging a bitter and unprofitable struggle against competitors in newly industrialized countries (NICs). While the shakeout is still going on, the management must already be thinking about what the company is going to do after its restructuring strategy has been accomplished.

The last of these examples prompts the general observation that the new patterns of competition now emerging in the world are not of academic interest alone, but are relevant to many industries. Investing in NICs to take advantage of their cheap labour is often a short-sighted solution: a company that does so may find, when its cost advantage has partly eroded away, that it is facing cut-throat competition from a heavily automated domestic industry that has evolved new patterns of production.

So let your thoughts fly a little way ahead of the airplane. The important thing is to give your thoughts time to coalesce into a structure capable of influencing the way you are heading.

Appendix: The basics of strategy

The model description given here does not pretend to cover all the models found in the field of strategy. It is however intended to give an outline of those models which have gained wider currency and thus constitute part of what everybody ought to know about strategy. Accordingly, some models with a technocratic bias have been omitted altogether, among them a number of three-dimensional matrices with assorted variables along their axes. Though these may have some uses, I myself have never come across them in actual business practice, and my impression is that they belong to the history of strategic development in the 1960s and early 1970s.

In the period since the Second World War, corporate strategies have been developed largely with a view to improving companies' long-term prospects for survival and profitability.

The emergence of strategy was based on three essential observations:

(a) It had been noted that operative skills were often associated with a lack of attention to long-term changes that affected business in a state of equilibrium.
(b) In diversified conglomerates, i.e. corporations comprising a wide variety of business units with little or nothing in common, a need was felt to find structures for managing a number of discrete business units (portfolio).
(c) The Second World War had focused attention on new types of control mechanisms based on operations research, queueing theory and advanced logistics, and it was assumed that these systems could be applied to private business enterprises.

If we view the development of strategy over an extended period, we can clearly see how much more some of the factors that determine success in business have changed.

In this Appendix, I shall briefly review some of the most widely used models, because they come under the heading of general strategic knowledge.

I have found a need, among companies interested in the

emergent subject of strategy, for access to short and concise explanations of the commonest models. The interested teacher or reader is of course free to investigate further, for there are plenty of other models about and, of course, much more detailed descriptions of the ones mentioned here.

During the economic expansion of the 1950s, corporate managements found themselves facing new problems and challenges. Companies were growing more diversified in their structures and were no longer great monolithic machines churning out a single product to satisfy a single need. At the same time, corporate managements were forced to make choices between alternative forms of growth in an economic climate where growth appeared to be constant and availability of capital limited. Many large companies at that time felt a need for techniques and instruments to help them deal with this situation. Thus arose what came to be called 'portfolio strategy'. The background was that new concepts were developed in the late 1950s to acquire a better grasp of investment in the stock market. People in the world of finance spoke of 'portfolios' of stocks. The term passed into general business parlance, where it was used to designate a group of variegated business units.

By the mid-1960s portfolio strategy had become a generally accepted method of measuring, comparing and assessing diversity. At about that time the General Electric Company began to feel the need for a better way to focus the attention of management on natural business within the framework of the diversified business that the company was – and still is – engaged in.

It was at General Electric that the concept of the 'strategic business unit' was first formulated. This concept was quickly adopted by other mammoth American corporations, and eventually became the basis of the wave of divisionalization that set the trend for business organization development in Europe in the 1970s and 1980s.

The Boston Consulting Group, founded and led by Bruce Henderson, was the first to develop a more systematic approach to these new concepts. Their main idea was that individual business units within a portfolio could be evaluated according to two criteria:

(a) growth of the market in which the business unit operated;
(b) the relative share of the market held by that particular business unit.

The conclusions subsequently drawn from these variables were based on something called the *experience curve*.

The experience curve

The experience curve was invented in 1925 by the Commanding Officer of the Wright-Patterson Air Force Base in Dayton, Ohio. He had observed that any operation could be performed at about 30% lower unit cost if the volume was doubled. This observation led to the formulation of the experience curve on which many of the older strategy models were based, including the BCG matrix. Figure A is a stylized representation of the Experience Curve.

The experience curve is mainly applicable to manufacturing operations. It is classic insofar as it constitutes the essence of the economy-of-scale philosophy that long dominated strategy development.

The theory implies that a large market share is valuable because it offers opportunities to increase production capacity and thus move down the experience curve in the direction of lower production costs. In this way you can achieve higher margins, better profitability and, consequently, a better competitive position.

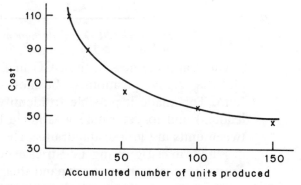

Fig. A The experience curve

The theory further suggests that accumulated production makes it possible to benefit from experience, which will gradually improve the efficiency of production. There is a constant teaching effect in addition to the opportunities to specialize and distribute capital costs over a larger number of manufactured units.

167

The BCG matrix

One of the most important developments in the evolution of strategy was the introduction of the two-dimensional matrix. By selecting factors judged to be crucial to management decision-making, such matrices can clarify the problems that management must solve. The first of these matrices to come into wide use was the Boston Consulting Group's growth/share matrix (Fig. B).

To use the BCG matrix, one plots the growth rate of a business unit's market on one axis (usually the vertical one), against the business unit's share of that market on the other axis. Most analysis consider absolute market share to be of secondary importance in this context, preferring to take the market share of the two to four largest competitors as the baseline. Relative market share is thus the most usual yardstick.

	Relative market share	
	High	Low
High	Star	Question mark
Low	Cash cow	Dog

Growth rate (vertical axis label)

Fig. B The BCG growth/share matrix

The real usefulness of the BCG matrix lay in using it to plot the relative positions of business units within a portfolio. This made it possible to identify 'winners' (market leaders) and to determine whether a balance existed between units in the four quadrants. The theory is that business units in fast-growing industries need a constant input of capital to enable them to expand their capacity. Business units in slow-growing industries, on the other hand, are expected to generate a positive cash flow.

This matrix was used chiefly as a way to assess the need for financing in diversified concerns. It did not attempt to explain the criteria for success or the state of competition in different industries, but was intended simply to help the managements of diversified groups manage their portfolios.

The theory implies that large corporations have a need to balance their portfolios by mixing business units that need capital to grow with units that generate capital.

This matrix undoubtedly owes much of its popularity to the names given to the four quadrants:

(a) Business units with a large market share in growth sectors are called *stars*;
(b) Units with a high market share in steady-state industries are called *cash cows*;
(c) Units with small market shares in fast-growing industries are called *question marks* (or *mavericks*);
(d) Units with a low market share in a stagnant market are called *dogs*.

The BCG matrix has subsequently come in for some hard, and to some extent justified, criticism. All attempts at model construction necessarily involve a skilful choice of simplifications, but in the light of today's knowledge the simplifications in the BCG matrix look far too sweeping.

Market attractiveness/strategic position

This concept was developed at roughly the same time by both the McKinsey Company and General Electric within the framework of the PIMS model. Unlike the BCG matrix, this concept aimed at a more considered assessment of the prospects of individual business units. A matrix of this kind as used by McKinsey is shown in Fig. C.

The methods of rating market attractiveness and strategic position vary somewhat. A special and very fundamental question is of course on what geographical market the relative market share should be calculated. There are plenty of examples on record of how misjudgements of market shares have led to disastrously bad decisions.

Some of the criteria used to judge strategic position and market attractiveness are listed overleaf:

Strategic position	Market attractiveness
Relative size	Absolute size
Growth	Market growth
Market share	Market breadth
Position	Pricing
Relative profitability	Structure of competition
Margin	Industry profitability
Technological position	Technical role
Image (reality as per-	Social role
ceived by outsiders)	Legal obstacles
Leadership and people	

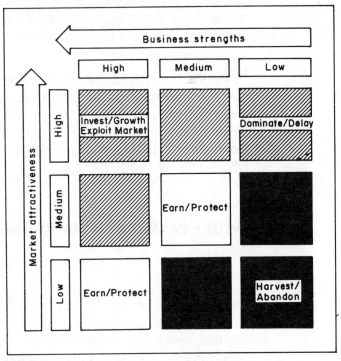

Fig. C Market attractiveness/strategic position matrix

These nine-field matrices have lately been very severely criticized. The criticism has focused mainly on the consequences of the recommendations that generally emanate from the use of these matrices.

For example; if a business unit is judged to be in a weak strategic position in an unattractive market, the theory says that it should be 'harvested', i.e. milked for every last drop of capital that can be wrung out of it, and then dropped. Following this advice has repeatedly proved disastrous. In the first place, who wants to be President of a company scheduled for rape and murder? General Electric, where

170

much of this kind of thinking originated, has now radically reappraised such broad recommendations. Manufacture of streetcars, transmission of DC power and other business operations held to be in a poor strategic position on unpromising markets have proved capable of achieving great successes where management did the opposite of what the model recommended. Thus for example the manufacture and sale of streetcars and subway systems has proved to have a great development potential, the simplistic recommendations of the model to the contrary notwithstanding.

The Mysigma profitability graph

The Swedish consultancy firm Mysigma specialize in capital rationalization, i.e. ways and means of minimizing the amount of capital tied up in inventory.

Mysigma has devised a graph of high explanatory value (Fig. D). It shows the relationship between profit margin on the one hand, and rate of capital turnover on the other. This graph admirably illustrates the value of simultaneously manipulating the three variables that determine profitability:

(a) reducing tied-up capital, thereby speeding capital turnover;
(b) reducing cost mass, thereby increasing profit margin;
(c) increasing profit margin by increasing prices.

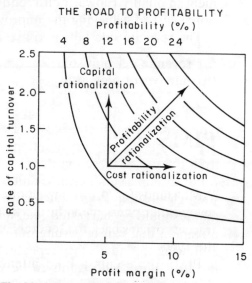

Fig. D The Mysigma profitability graph

171

There are three kinds of capital:

(a) fixed assets;
(b) inventory;
(c) bills receivable.

Cash management theory has long provided a variety of suggestions for dealing with bills receivable. Mysigma's approach is based on cutting down on the capital tied up in inventory. And lately there has been a growth of interest in fixed asset capital, of which real estate is an important component.

The cost side of the graph comprises:

(a) variable unit costs, dependent on the volume of production;
(a) capacity costs, independent of the volume of production.

The latter category generally includes interest on fixed assets, while the former includes interest on inventory and bills receivable.

Manipulating the value variable in an attempt to increase revenues more than the added cost of added value is generally called business development. It actually involves businesslike risk-taking, and has been a subject of attention in recent years. Research, using the PIMS database and other sources, has shown that an improvement in customer-perceived quality is reflected by an increase in margins. This means that the additional revenue earned by an improvement in quality (upward differentiation) exceeds the additional cost of achieving the improvement.

The revenue side falls into two parts:

(a) revenue per unit sold;
(b) number of units sold.

PIMS

PIMS stands for 'profit impact of marketing strategy'. Like many other phenomena in the field of strategy, PIMS can trace its origins back to General Electric in the latter half of the 1960s.

PIMS represents a bold attempt to synthesize all the

variables that affect a company's long-term profitability. Based on some thirty variables, it claims to be able to give 67% of the total explanation of a company's success.

PIMS consists of a database covering nearly 3000 business units, mainly in North American and European companies. It contains all the variables on each of these companies, and by subscribing to PIMS you can compare business units in your own sphere of activity with the strategic guidelines given in the empirical PIMS material. The fact that the model *is* empirical is one of the great advantages of PIMS: this narrows the gap between the abstract and the concrete.

PIMS divides the causal factors into the three groups shown in Fig. E.

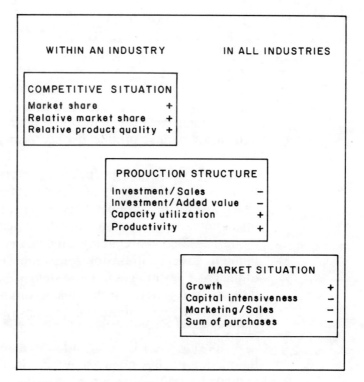

Fig. E Decisive profitability factors according to PIMS

As the figure shows, *competitive situation* refers to market share (both absolute and relative) and relative product quality, which is measured on the basis of both service and product variables.

Production structure refers to the amount of tied-up capital in relation to sales and in relation to added value. These factors are followed by minus signs, meaning that an increasing amount of tied-up capital relative to sales or added value results in declining profitability. Other causal variables under this heading are capacity utilization and productivity measured in terms of added value.

Market situation refers to the growth of the market, the capital intensiveness of the industry (which has a negative influence on profitability), marketing costs relative to the value of sales, and the total amount spent on purchasing. A high purchase sum generally has a negative effect on profitability.

The factors that have the greatest influence on profitability are

(a) capital intensiveness
(b) relative product quality
(c) relative market share
(d) productivity

in that order.

An attractive feature of the PIMS model is that it attempts to measure relative product quality. As readers of this book will have gathered, I am convinced that the key to success in business lies in the fulfilment of customers' need structures. PIMS is the only strategy analysis system that attempts to chart how far the product satisfies need structures, except for Michael Porter's value chain (see next section).

The PIMS database is currently operated by the Strategic Planning Institute in Boston, with branches elsewhere. One of the great advantages of the system is the high level of the discussions it generates: the conclusions may sometimes be too hastily drawn, but the debate is always on the right level and concerned with essentials.

A drawback to PIMS, or rather to its interpreters, is the temptation to get caught up in a mechanistic view of companies and their development and forget the realities of business. One finds that people with a bias towards technocratic planning sometimes have a weakness for PIMS, to the detriment of the system's reputation among more business-oriented strategies.

But there is another great advantage of PIMS that must be emphasized, namely the rich body of research that is being done on the material in the PIMS database. This research is generating new ideas on many important facets of strategy.

174

Porter's generative strategies

The term 'generative' means universally applicable or derived from certain basic postulates.

Michael Porter has written two well-known books, *Competitive Strategy* and *Competitive Advantage*. In the latter, he has further pursued his line of thinking about the model for generative strategies illustrated in Fig. F.

		Lower cost	Differentiation
COMPETITIVE SCOPE	Broad target	1. Cost leadership	2. Differentiation
	Narrow target	3A. Cost focus	3B. Differentiation focus

Fig. F Generative strategy model

The idea behind the generative strategy concept is that competitive advantage is the true heart of all strategies. To achieve a competitive advantage, a company must make a choice to avoid becoming 'all things to all men'.

Cost leadership is the most distinct of the three generative strategies. It means that the company aims to be the low-cost producer in its industry. The company has a broad scope of delivery and serves many segments within its industry.

Differentiation means that the company strives to be unique in its industry in some respect that is important to buyers. Differentiation can be sought in the product itself, in the system of delivery, or in some other of the company's various functions. The road to differentiation is beset with pitfalls and must therefore be trodden with extreme care and a high degree of creativity.

Focus is Porter's team for choosing a segment within an industry and devising a strategy for that segment. A good example is the special car segment of the automotive industry, where Volvo has elected to focus on estate cars and leads the whole industry in that field.

Structural analysis of industries

The model in Fig. G, developed by Michael Porter, takes in the five competitive forces that determine profitability in an industry.

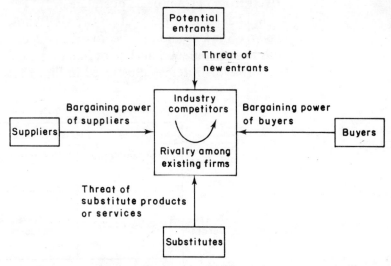

Fig. G The five competitive forces

Competitive strategies (business strategies) are derived from an understanding of the rules of competition that govern an industry and determine its attractiveness. The ultimate goal of competitive strategy is to influence those rules in one's own company's favour.

The rules of competition can be described by the five competitive forces shown in the figure. They are:

(a) entry of new competitiors into the arena;
(b) the threat from substitutes, i.e. the satisfaction of customers' needs by other technology;
(c) the bargaining power of buyers;
(d) the bargaining power of suppliers;
(e) competition between companies already established in the industry.

The generic value chain

The value chain, developed by Michael Porter and illustrated in its generic form in Fig. H, represents one of the first serious attempts in the field of strategy to analyse customer need structures. However, it deals exclusively with the

176

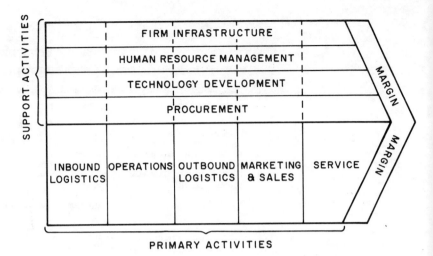

Fig. H The generic value chain

rational aspects of need structures, ignoring the subtle influences exercised by emotionally based value judgements.

Value is defined in this context as what buyers are willing to pay for what they get from suppliers. A company is profitable if the value it generates exceeds the cost it has to pay for generating the value. The goal of every strategy is to produce a value to the buyer greater than the cost of producing the value. Analysis of the competitive situation must therefore be based not on cost, but on value.

Porter divides value into *primary activities* and *support activities*. Figure H shows the primary values at the bottom, listing them as inbound logistics, operations, outbound logistics, marketing (i.e. creation of demand), sales and service. The term 'support activities' refers to the corporate infrastructure as shown in the figure.

Anyone interested in further studies of the value chain should read Porter's book *Competitive Advantage*, which deals largely with that very subject.

GAP analysis

GAP analysis was developed at the Stanford Research Institute. It can be characterized as an attempt to find a method of dealing with strategy development and managing one's way to a higher level of ambition.

Fig. 1 GAP analysis

Performance goals and portfolio strategy

1. Formulate preliminary performance goals for one year, three years and five years.

2. Forecast profit development relative to currently set goals for existing business units.

3. Establish gap between goals and forecasts.

4. Identify other investment alternatives for each business unit and forecast results.

5. Identify general alternative competitive positions for each business unit and forecast results.

6. Discuss investments and business strategy alternatives for each business unit.

7. Arrive at a synthesis of the portfolio perspective with reference to goal strategy for each business unit.

8. Establish gap between preliminary performance target and forecast for each business unit.

9. Specify profile of possible business unit acquisitions.

10. Determine resources required to make such acquisitions and effect on existing business units.

11. Revise goals and strategies of existing business units with a view to creating these resources.

12. Establish a synthesis that determines goals and strategies.

The steps in a GAP analysis are given in Fig. I. This particular example refers to a portfolio analysis, i.e. a group of business units, but similar schemes have also been developed for dealing with individual business units.

As the figure indicates, GAP analysis can be described as an organized attack on the gap between desired and predicted performance.

The product/market matrix

The PM matrix has been in use for a long time and still has extensive practical applications. An astonishing degree of ignorance prevails in many companies concerning their customer segments and the products offered to each segment. Simply listing products (range of goods and services) and markets (different categories of buyers) often provides valuable insights that can prompt changes in a product portfolio, development of a new product range or establishment of successful business strategies. Figure J shows the product/market matrix in its simplest form.

Customer segment \ Product	1	2	3	4
A				
B				

Fig. J Product/market matrix

Problem detection studies

The problem detection study (PDS) technique cannot really be called a strategy model, but it does play a decisive part in the current trend of strategic thinking towards a deep understanding of customer need structures.

The PDS process (Fig. K) involves starting with a number of in-depth interviews in order to formulate the problems connected with the use of a given product or service. The rough list of problems is then used as a basis for polling a large number of respondents. The responses are crunched in a computer and then classified in various ways on the basis of the problem areas.

Although this technique does not get to the root of customer need structures, it does often offer a good grasp of the problems that customers experience in using a particular product or service. The results of a problem detection study can often be utilized to make a company more competitive.

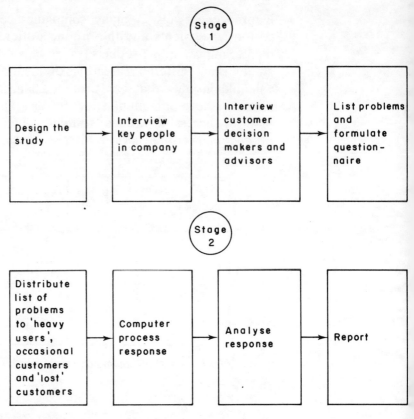

Fig. K The PDS process

McKinsey's 7S model*

McKinsey's 7S model cannot really be considered as a pure strategy model, but rather as a way of thinking about the development or remodelling of organizations. Its name comes from the seven factors that McKinsey found essential in the context of organization development: strategy, skills, shared values, structure, systems, staff and style (Fig. L).

We can sum up the model by saying that McKinsey felt it was important that all seven factors should be taken into consideration whenever a change in organization is contemplated. There are innumerable examples of attempted changes that have failed through neglecting to address one or more of these factors.

Normally, when a company sets out to change its organization, the seven S's are dealt with in a given sequence. In the first phase the strategy is usually determined. The

---

* Source: Dag Sundström, McKinsey & Company Inc., Stockholm.

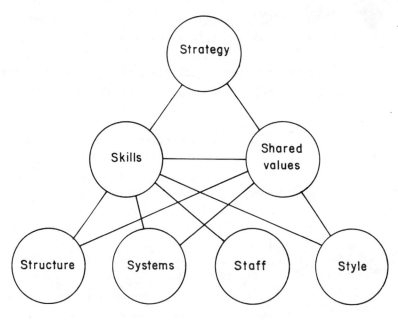

Fig. L McKinsey's 7S model

next step is to define what the organization must be specially good at in order to be able to implement its strategy, i.e. what *skills* it must develop or otherwise acquire. The final step is to determine what changes are needed in the other five factors to make the change a successful one.

Strategy describes where the company or business unit should concentrate its forces and compete, and what coordinated actions must be taken to achieve a sustained competitive edge. Strategy, in other words, answers the questions of where the company should compete and how.

Assuming one has a clear idea of a suitable strategy for the company, the next step is to decide what essential *skills* the new strategy calls for. The strategy tells the company how it must adapt itself to its environment and use its organizational potential, whereas the analysis of skills answers the question of how the strategy ought to be implemented. It is seldom difficult to define five, or maybe even ten skills of fundamental importance. But this is not enough, because the need is to develop *winning* skills, and this often makes such heavy demands on the organization that it is only possible to develop between one and three skills concurrently. These skills represent the link between the strategy and the new era, while at the same time they define the changes that need to be made in the other five S's: structure, systems, staff, style and shared values.

A company's *structure* is perhaps the best known of the concepts relating to organizational change. It refers to the way business areas, divisions and units are grouped in relation to each other. This, too, is perhaps the most visible factor in the organization, and that is why it is often tempting to begin by changing the structure. There are many examples of corporate managements who thought they could reorganize their companies through structural changes.

Systems can be defined as the routines or processes which exist in a company and which involve many people for the purpose of identifying important issues, getting things done or making decisions. Systems have a very strong influence on what happens in most organizations, and provide management with a powerful tool for making changes in the organization.

The *staff* factor is concerned with the question of what kind of people the company needs. This is not so much a question of single individuals as of the total know-how possessed by the people in the organization.

Style is one of the lesser-known implements in the management toolbox. It can be said to consist of two elements: personal time and symbolic actions. Thus management style is not a matter of personal style, but of what the executives in the organization do: how do they use their personal signal system?

Shared values, finally, refer to one or more guiding themes of the organization – things that everybody is aware of as being specially important and crucial to the survival and success of the organization.

As we have seen, skills are the integrating factor in the 7S model. According to this model, when you think of organizational change you start by thinking about strategy, and on the basis of that strategy you define the most important skills you need before proceeding to decide what changes are necessary in the other factors in the 7S model.

The 7S model has often been misinterpreted, and has consequently been applied in an imprecise fashion. This model does not in fact pretend to be a guide to the development of either business or portfolio strategies, but simply represents a holistic view of corporate development. The fact that some people are put off by acronyms should not be allowed to obscure the model's explanatory value.

Bibliography

Abell, D.E. and Hammond, J.S., *Strategic Market Planning: Problems and Analytical Approaches*, Prentice-Hall, New Jersey, 1979.

Adizes, I., *Ledarskapets fallgropar*, Liber, Stockholm, 1979.

Andersson, R., Bergkvist, T., Bruzelius, L.H., Dahlman, C., Lundahl, V. and Åkesson, G., *Krävande företagsledning*, Liber, Lund 1982.

Ansoff, H.I., *Checklist for Competitive and Competence Profiles*, Corporate strategy, pp. 98–99, New York, McGraw-Hill, 1965.

Brandes, O. and Breges, S., *Strategy Development in Swedish Multinational Companies*, Prince Bertil's Symposium, 1984.

Chandler, A.D., *Strategy and Structure*, MIT Press, USA, 1962.

Deal, T.E. and Kennedy, A.A., Corporate Cultures, Timo, Vänersborg, 1983.

Drucker, P.F., *Managing for Result*, Wahlström & Widstrand, Stockholm, 1970.

Edgren, J., Rhenman, E. and Skärvad, P.-H., *Divisionalisering och därefter*, Management Media, Stockholm, 1983.

Engellau, P., *Påhittigheten blockerad? – en studie av innovationsklimatet i Sverige*, Sekretariatet för framtidsstudier, Liber, Trosa, 1979.

Friman, A., *Marknadsundersökningar som Idésökare Eller Knotroll*, Back, R. (ed), Marknadsföring, Norstedt, Lund, 1978.

Fruhan, W.E., Jr, *The Fight for Competitive Advantage*, Cambridge, Mass.: Division of Research, Harvard Graduate School for Business Administration, 1972.

Galbraith, J.R. and Nathanson, D.A., *Strategy Implementation: The Role of Structure and Process*, West Publishing Co., USA, 1980.

Grönroos, C., *Marknadsföring av tjänster*, Akademi-litteratur/MCT/Svenska Handelshögskolan Helsingfors, Stockholm, 1979.

Grönroos, C., *Marknadsföring i tjänsteföretag*, Liber, Stockholm, 1983b.

Hammarkvist, K.-O., Håkansson, H. and Mattsson, L.-G., *Marknadsföring för konkurrenskraft*, Liber, Kristiandstad, 1982.

Harrigan, K.R., *Strategies for Declining Industries*, DBA Avhandling, Harvard Graduate School of Business Administration, 1979.

Haspelagh, P., *Portfolio Planning; Uses and Limits*, Harvard Business Review, Jan–Feb, 1982.

Henderson, B, *The experience curve*, review, Boston Consulting Group, USA, 1977.

183

Hickman, C.R. and Silva, M.A., *Creating Excellence, 1984*, Excellence Malmö, Liber, 1986.

Hofstede, G., *Culture's Consequences*, Sage Publications, USA, 1980.

Karlöf, B., *Affärsutveckling*, IBM, Göteborg, 1983.

Kotler, P., *Marketing Management*, Prentice-Hall, USA, 1980.

Laurelli, R., *TOTAL-säljaren*, Studentlitteratur, Lund, 1979.

Lekvall, P. and Wahlbin, C., *Information för marknadsförings-beslut*, IHM, Göteborg.

Levitt, T, *The Marketing Imagination*, Free Press, USA, 1983, 'Exploit the Product Life Cycle'. Harvard Business Review, November/December 1965, pp. 81–94.

Lorange, P. and Vancil, R.F., *Strategic Planning Systems*, Prentice-Hall, USA, 1977.

Mintzberg, H., *Planning on the Left Side and Managing on the Right*, Harvard Business Review, July–August 1976, Strategy in Three Modes. California Management Review, 1984.

Naisbitt, J., *Megatrends*, Warner Books, USA, 1982.

Newman, H.H., *Strategic Groups and the Structure–Performance Relationship*, Review of Economics and Statistics, Arg. LX, August 1978, pp. 417–427.

Normann, R., *Skapande företagsledning*, Aldus, Lund, 1976.

Normann, R., *Service Management*, Liber, Malmö, 1983.

Ohmae, K., *The Mind of the Strategist – The Art of Japanese Business*, McGraw-Hill, USA, 1982.

Peters, T.J. and Waterman, R.H., Jr, *In Search of Excellence*, Harper & Row, USA, 1982.

Porter, E., *Competitive Strategy*, Free Press, USA, 1980.

Rotschild, W.E., *Putting it all Together*, Amacom, New York; 1979.

Schelling, T., *The Strategy of Conflict*, Harvard University Press, Cambridge Mass., 1960.

Simon, H.A., *On the Concept of Organizational Goal*, Ansoff, H.I. (ed.), Business Strategy, Middlesex, 1971.

Sjöstrand, S.-E., *Organisationsteorier*, Studentlitteratur, Lund, 1979.

Steiner, G., *Strategic Planning*, Collier Macmillan, 1979.

af Trolle, U., *Strategi för ny välfärd*, Liber, Kristianstad, 1978.

Tuvfesson, I., Towards a new interpretation of marketing management, in *Trends in Management and Management Development*, MIL/Studentlitteratur, Lund, 1982.

Yavitz, B. and Newman, B., *Strategy in Action*, Free Press, 1983.

Zimmerman, T., *Top Management Strategy – What it is and How to Make it Work*, Simon & Schuster, 1981.

Österman, E., *Handbok för industriell kampanjplanering*, Liber, Stockholm, 1982.